Mel Bay's Deluxe

Harmonica Method

A Thorough Study for the Individual or Group

By Phil Duncan

A recording and video of the music in this book are now available. The publisher strongly recommends the use of these resources along with the text to insure accuracy of interpretation and ease in learning.

Foreword

To the student:

This book is designed as a thorough step by step instruction on the "10" hole harmonica. This comprehensive book explains musical techniques with playing techniques. The playing of the "10" hole harmonica can be achieved by playing each song and exercise as presented in this book. This book's purpose is to help combat the trial and error of playing the harmonica, and puts the playing of the harmonica in the reach of everyone. It is suggested by the author that each harmonica student seek out a music instructor to further help eliminate errors.

Philip Duncan

To the teacher:

This book will guide the harmonica teacher, or, in fact, any music teacher, with exercises and an array of pieces that have been adapted specifically for the "10" hole harmonica. It is surprising that in the long history of harmonica; the teaching of harmonica as "formal education" is still controversial. In bygone days the harmonica player gained experience in the everyday challenges of creating music. He learned from his fellow players and he had time for trial and error while trying out new ideas at the risk of failing. But with the fast pace of today these opportunities are virtually non-existent. In any event, a book such as this one fills the gap by organizing the "learning process" by steps so as to minimize the errors on the road to achievement. With the guidance of a music teacher the errors can virtually be eliminated.

Philip Duncan

Musical Contents

Introduction

There are two types of harmonicas, the chromatic and diatonic. This book will use the diatonic harmonica ONLY. Specifically, it will use the TEN-HOLE Harmonica in the key of "C".

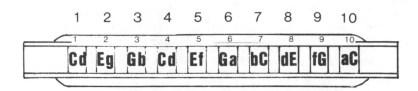

How To Hold The Harmonica

Hold the harmonica firmly in the left hand with hole number one to the left. The left index and middle fingers should lie along the upper part of the instrument and the thumb along the lower part. The right hand should be cupped around the back side of the harmonica.

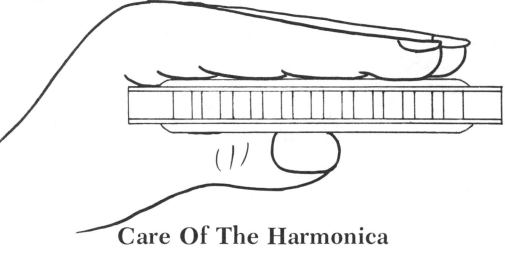

Care Of The Harmonica

Depending on how much it is used, the instrument will eventually deteriorate and some of the reeds will either get stuck or play out of tune. If you live in a big city you may find a repair shop that can restore a worn out harmonica. Probably it would be best, however, just to purchase a new one.

Carefully avoid playing the harmonica after eating. Food particles will stop the reeds from playing. Always slap the harmonica on the palm of the hand to clear any saliva or foreign particles that may be in the instrument. Many players soak their harmonicas in water before playing. This makes wood harmonicas swell, giving an air tight fit. This means that more sound can be produced with less effort. After the instrument is soaked, the excess water must be removed by tapping the harmonica on the palm of the hand. Repeated soaking of the wood harmonicas will cause the wood parts to swell permanently. It will be necessary to trim the wood that comes in contact with the mouth. This can be done with a sharp knife.

Producing The Single Tone

Sounds are produced by blowing the breath through the instrument or by drawing the breath through the instrument. To produce a single tone, place the harmoica comfortably in your mouth as though to blow four holes. Now bring your tongue forward so that it covers three holes on the left.* This should leave only one hole at the right of your mouth uncovered. Make sure you don't blow into more than one hole at a time. Keep your lips and tongue in the same position and blow, then draw the breath. DON'T LET AIR ESCAPE THROUGH THE SIDES OF YOUR MOUTH. BLOW AND DRAW T-H-R-O-U-G-H the harmonica not at it.

*Note: Place tongue on __ALL__ Holes, then move the tongue to the left until __ONE__ single tone is produced.

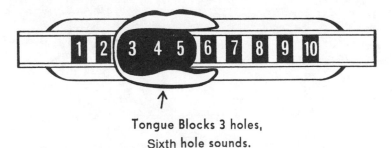

Tongue Blocks 3 holes,
Sixth hole sounds.

Vibrato

You may change the sound of your playing by adding a wavering tone, called VIBRATO. Holding the harmonica in the left hand, close the right hand over the left and by opening and closing the right hand, the wavering of the tone will begin. As the right hand is moved to and from, slowly, a rich mellow vibrato is the result. By moving the right hand quickly the wavering of the tone increases. The heel of both hands stay in contact with each other while the fingers of the right hand move back and forth in unison. The movement of the fingers should be smooth and even.

Example

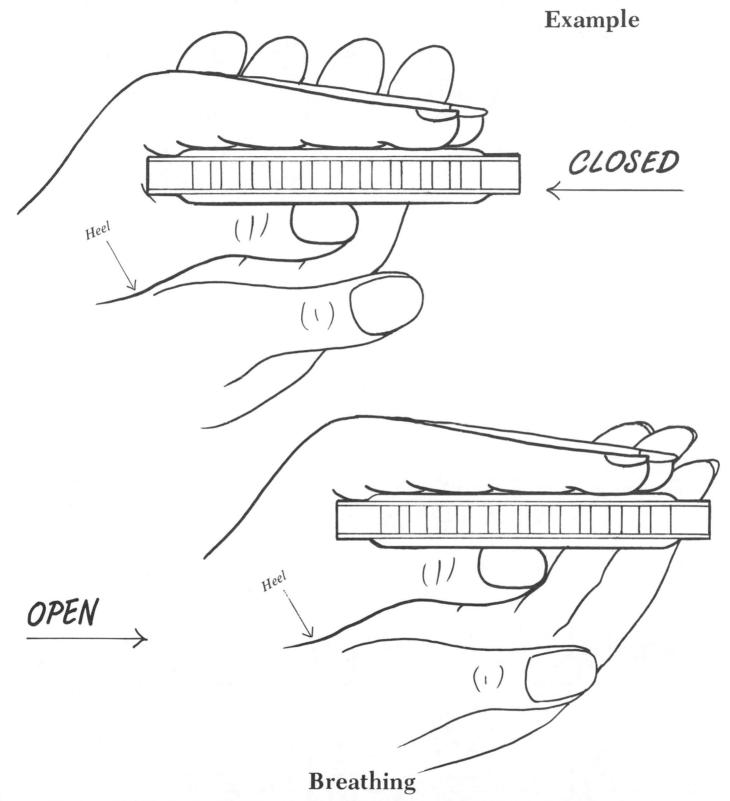

CLOSED ←

Heel

OPEN →

Heel

Breathing

The key to breathing is to breathe like a swimmer. In other words, you should breathe in the mouth and out the nose. This helps to exhale the excess air in your lungs on difficult passages. Don't let air escape through the sides of your mouth. Aim your breath THROUGH the harmonica not at it. You are ready for the excercises and pieces on the following pages. NOTE: Always COUNT THE TIME (Beats per measure) REMEMBER TO TAP YOUR FOOT TO EACH BEAT.

Chapter I
Music for the "10" Hole Harmonica

HARMONICA MUSIC IS
WRITTEN IN THE "G" OR
TREBLE CLEF.

THE MUSIC STAFF

Staff

Some notes
are line notes

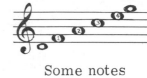

space
above

space
below

Some notes
are space notes

All notes are either line notes or space notes

Study the following notes and mark them ⬜L or ⬜S for line or space.

Study the following notes and write the number of the line or space.

6

This is a whole note. **o** In most music the whole note recieves 4 counts or beats. The sound must last 4 counts or beats.

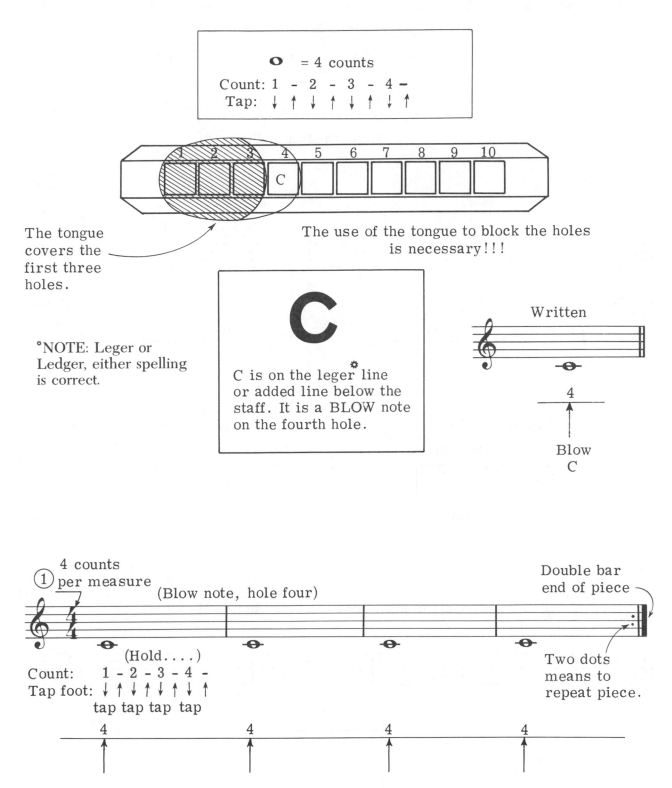

o = 4 counts

Count: 1 - 2 - 3 - 4 -
Tap: ↓ ↑ ↓ ↑ ↓ ↑ ↓ ↑

The tongue covers the first three holes.

The use of the tongue to block the holes is necessary!!!

°NOTE: Leger or Ledger, either spelling is correct.

C

C is on the leger° line or added line below the staff. It is a BLOW note on the fourth hole.

Written

4

Blow
C

① 4 counts per measure

(Blow note, hole four)

Double bar end of piece

(Hold....)

Count: 1 - 2 - 3 - 4 -
Tap foot: ↓ ↑ ↓ ↑ ↓ ↑ ↓ ↑
tap tap tap tap

Two dots means to repeat piece.

4   4   4   4

7

This is a half note. ♩ In most music the half note recieves 2 counts or beats. The sound must last 2 counts or beats.

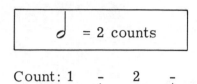

= 2 counts

Count: 1   -   2   -
Tap foot:↓   ↑   ↓   ↑

Down Up Down Up

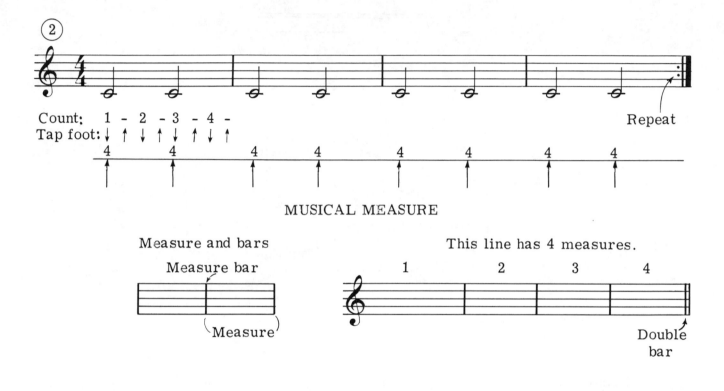

②

Count: 1 - 2 - 3 - 4 -
Tap foot: ↓ ↑ ↓ ↑ ↓ ↑ ↓ ↑

4   4   4   4   4   4   4   4

Repeat

MUSICAL MEASURE

Measure and bars

Measure bar

Measure

This line has 4 measures.

1   2   3   4

Double
bar

How many measures are there in this line?

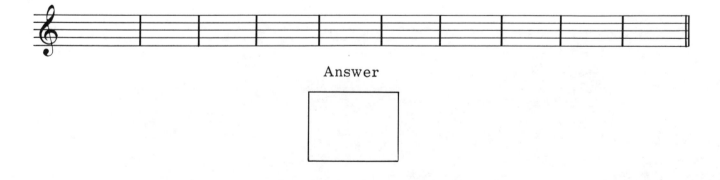

Answer

The tongue covers the first three holes.

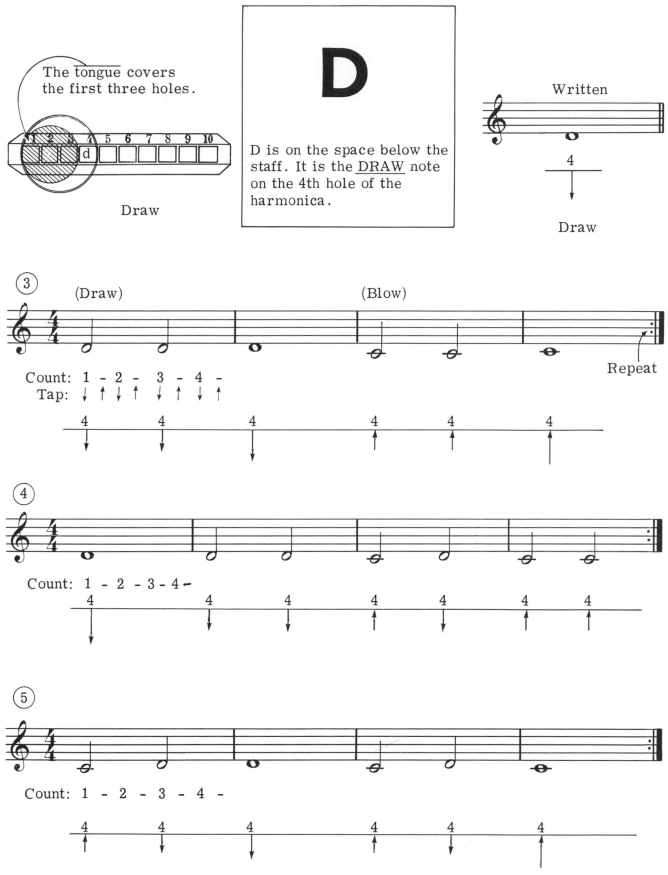

Draw

D

D is on the space below the staff. It is the DRAW note on the 4th hole of the harmonica.

Written

4
↓

Draw

③ (Draw)   (Blow)

Count: 1 - 2 - 3 - 4 -
Tap: ↓ ↑ ↓ ↑ ↓ ↑ ↓ ↑

4   4   4   4   4   4
↓   ↓   ↓   ↑   ↑   ↑

Repeat

④

Count: 1 - 2 - 3 - 4 -

4   4   4   4   4   4   4
↓   ↓   ↓   ↑   ↓   ↑   ↑

⑤

Count: 1 - 2 - 3 - 4 -

4   4   4   4   4   4
↑   ↓   ↓   ↑   ↓   ↑

REMEMBER: ALWAYS TAP THE FOOT!

This is a quarter note. ♩ In most music the quarter note recieves one count or beat. The sound lasts only one count or beat.

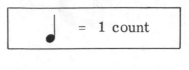

= 1 count

Count: 1 -
Tap foot: ↓ ↑

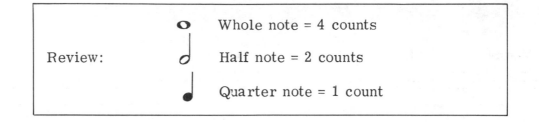

Review:

Whole note = 4 counts

Half note = 2 counts

Quarter note = 1 count

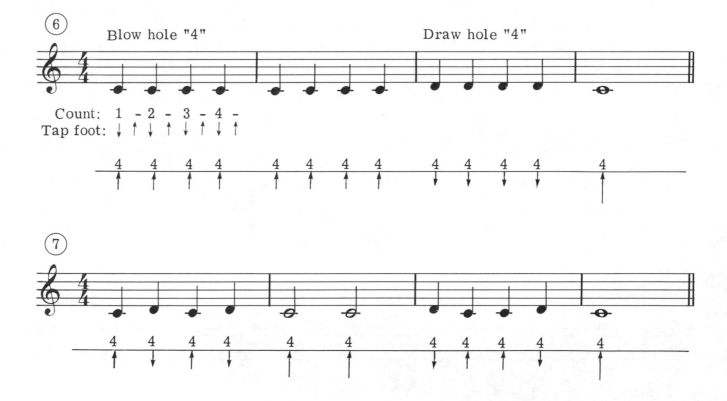

⑥ Blow hole "4"   Draw hole "4"

Count: 1 - 2 - 3 - 4 -
Tap foot: ↓ ↑ ↓ ↑ ↓ ↑ ↓ ↑

⑦

Quarter Rest

⑧ The quarter rest is one count of silence. (No air through the harmonica)

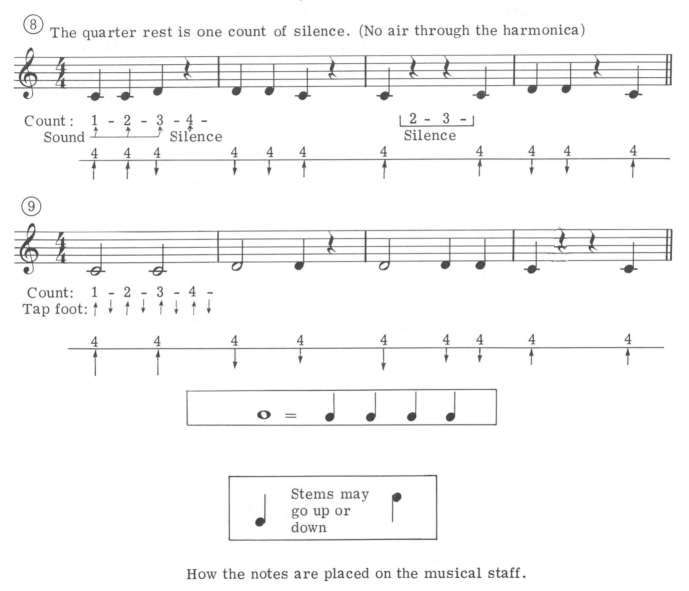

Count: 1 - 2 - 3 - 4 -
Sound   Silence |2 - 3 -| Silence

⑨

Count: 1 - 2 - 3 - 4 -
Tap foot: ↑ ↓ ↑ ↓ ↑ ↓ ↑ ↓

Stems may go up or down

How the notes are placed on the musical staff.

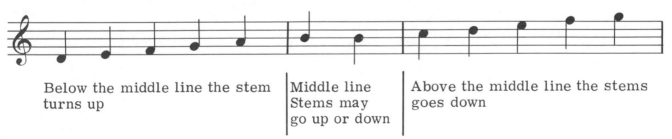

Below the middle line the stem turns up | Middle line Stems may go up or down | Above the middle line the stems goes down

Change these whole notes to quarter notes:

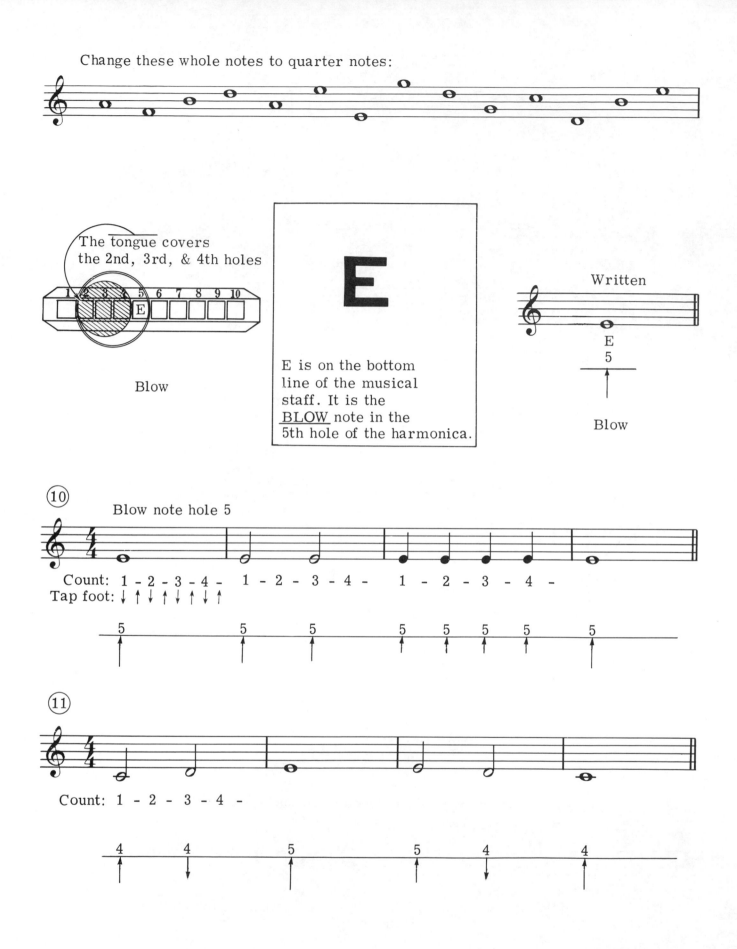

The tongue covers
the 2nd, 3rd, & 4th holes

Blow

E

E is on the bottom
line of the musical
staff. It is the
BLOW note in the
5th hole of the harmonica.

Written

E
5

Blow

⑩ Blow note hole 5

Count: 1 - 2 - 3 - 4 -   1 - 2 - 3 - 4 -   1 - 2 - 3 - 4 -
Tap foot: ↓ ↑ ↓ ↑ ↓ ↑ ↓ ↑

5   5   5   5   5   5   5   5

⑪

Count: 1 - 2 - 3 - 4 -

4   4   5   5   4   4

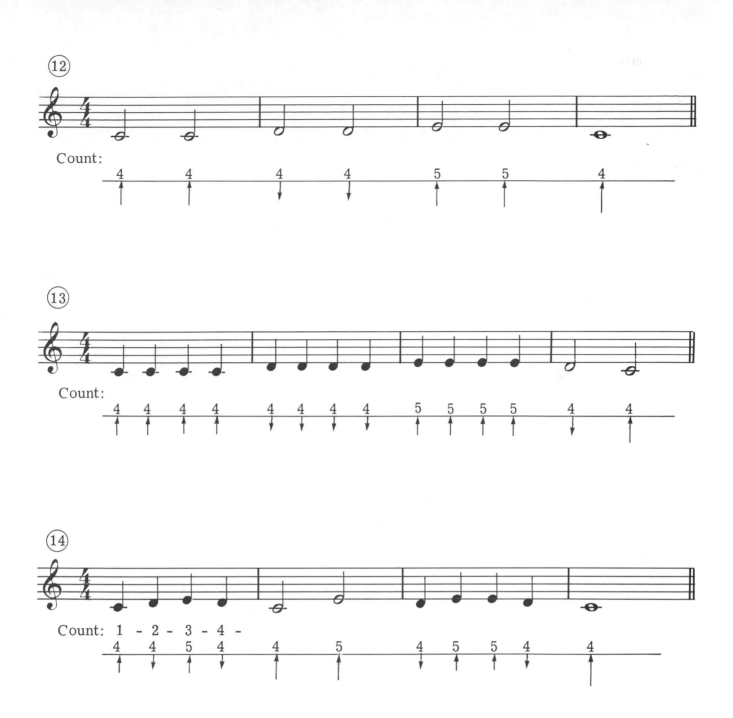

Hot Cross Buns [*]

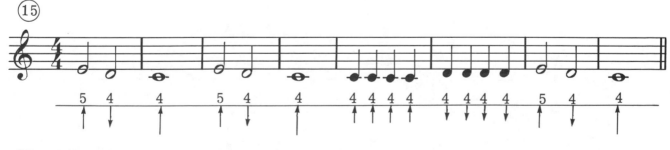

*See pages 104-107

Chapter II
Mary's Lamb

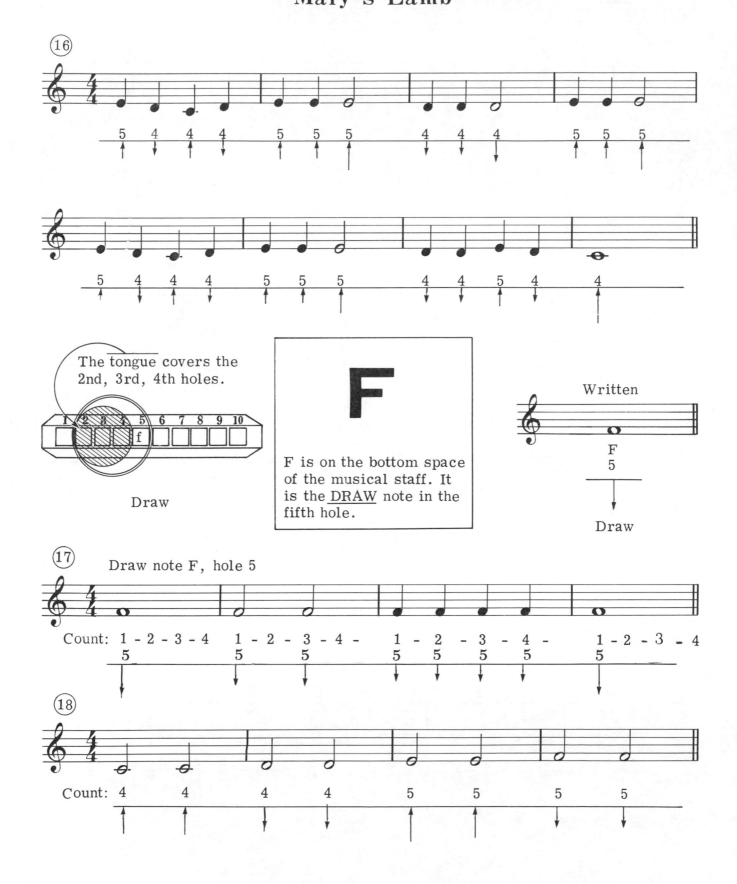

The tongue covers the 2nd, 3rd, 4th holes.

Draw

F

F is on the bottom space of the musical staff. It is the DRAW note in the fifth hole.

Written

F
5

Draw

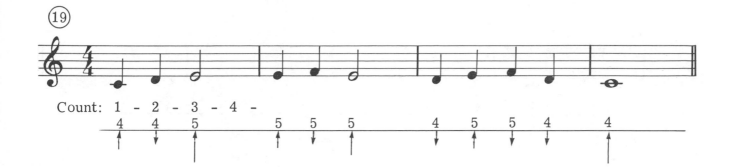

Count: 1 - 2 - 3 - 4 -

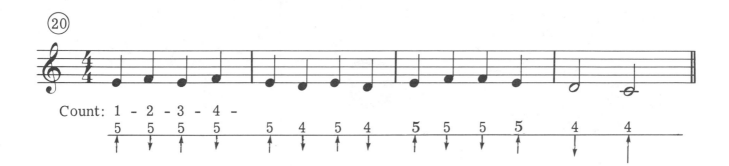

Count: 1 - 2 - 3 - 4 -

Dotted Half Note

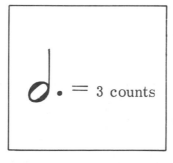

This is a dotted half note. ♩. In most music the dotted half note receives $\frac{3}{}$ counts.

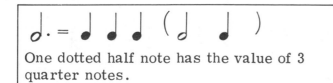

One dotted half note has the value of 3 quarter notes.

Count: 1 - 2 - 3 - 4 -
Tap: ↓ ↑ ↓ ↑ ↓ ↑ ↓ ↑

The tongue covers the 3rd, 4th and 5th holes.

Blow

G

G is on the second line of the musical staff. It is the **BLOW** note in the 6th hole.

Written

G

Blow

Note Values

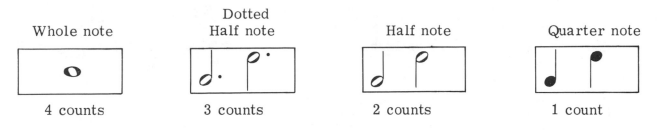

Whole note	Dotted Half note	Half note	Quarter note
4 counts	3 counts	2 counts	1 count

Fill in each box with the correct kind of note. Use [Q] for quarter note: [H] for the half note; [DH] for dotted half note; [W] for whole notes.

Fill in each box with the correct note value. (Number of counts)

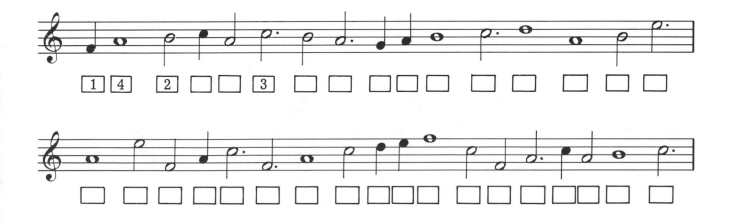

Time Signature

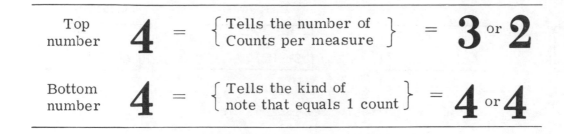

Top number	**4** = { Tells the number of Counts per measure }	=	**3** or **2**
Bottom number	**4** = { Tells the kind of note that equals 1 count }	=	**4** or **4**

(24)

Count: 1 - 2 - 3 - 1 - 2 - 3 - 1 - 2 - 3 - 1 - 2 - 3 -

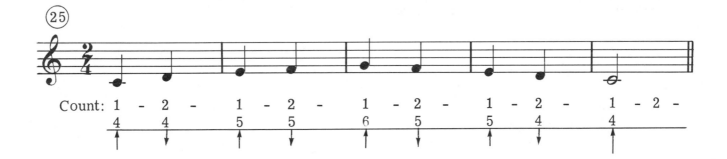

(25)

Count: 1 - 2 - 1 - 2 - 1 - 2 - 1 - 2 - 1 - 2 -

(26)

Count: 1 - 2 - 3 - 4 -

IMPORTANT!
ALWAYS PLAY TO YOUR TAPPING.

Some Folks Do

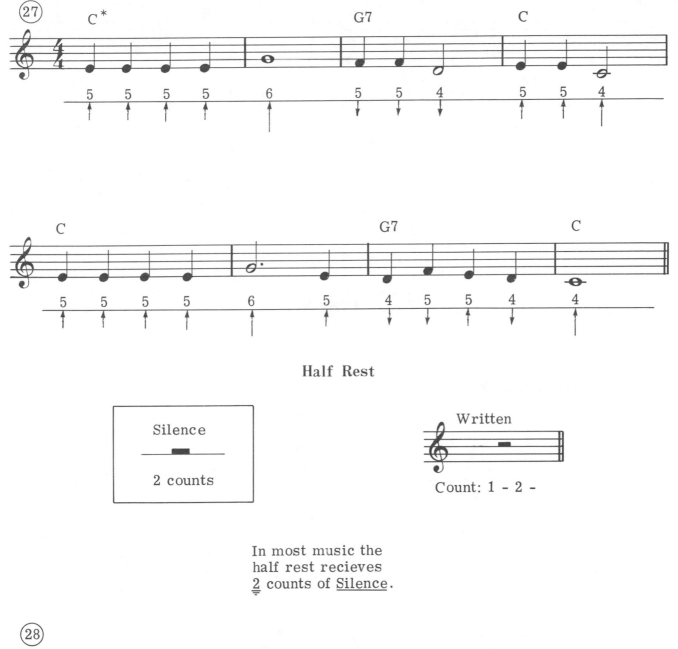

Half Rest

Silence
▬
2 counts

Written

Count: 1 - 2 -

In most music the
half rest recieves
$\frac{2}{\equiv}$ counts of <u>Silence</u>.

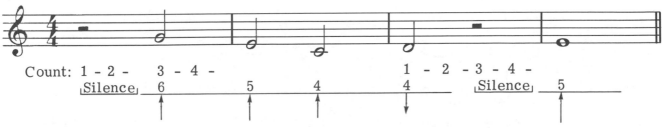

Count: 1 - 2 -   3 - 4 -   1 - 2 - 3 - 4 -
⌊Silence⌋   6   5   4   4   ⌊Silence⌋   5

* Chords for Guitar accompaniment

First and second endings were created to shorten the printing of music.

I Know Where I'm Going

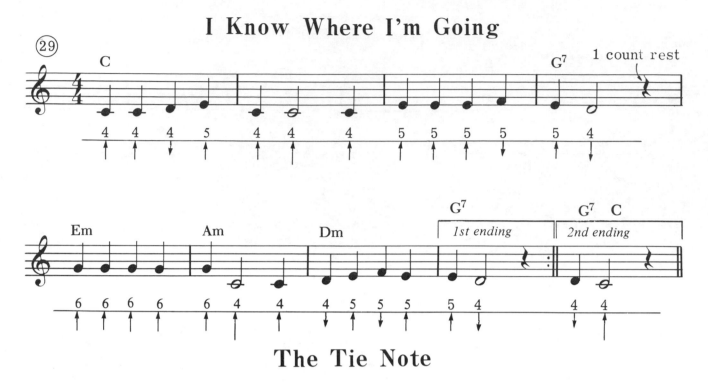

The Tie Note

The tie note is two or more notes of the same pitch that increase the length of sound.

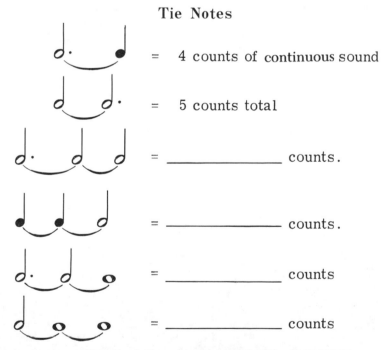

Tie Notes

= 4 counts of continuous sound

= 5 counts total

= _____ counts.

= _____ counts.

= _____ counts

= _____ counts

The first tie note is sounded and the second is held. <u>DO NOT</u> resound the second note, only hold it out for total value of both notes.

The first measure has only 3 counts. It begins with the second count. The first count may be found in the last measure.

When the Saints Go Marching In

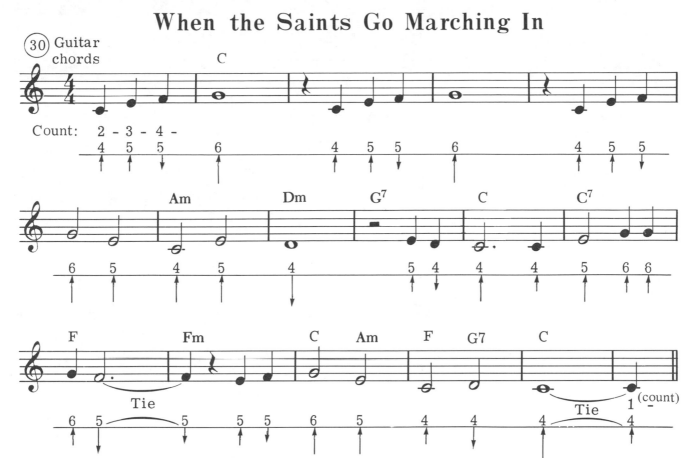

Ode to Joy

Beethoven

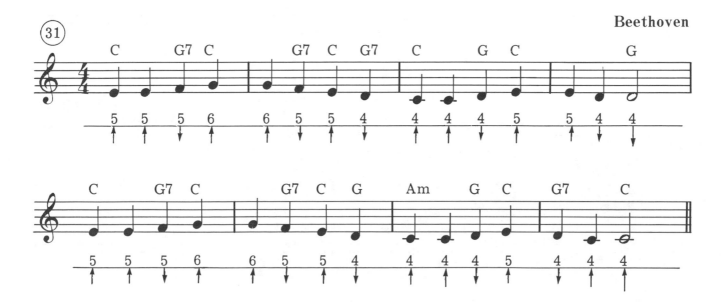

Jingle Bells

Waltzing

Chapter III

The tongue covers the 3rd, 4th & 5th hole

Draw

A

A is on the second space of the musical staff. It is a DRAW note on the 6th hole.

Written

A
6

Draw

Count: 1 - 2 - 3 - 4 - 1 - 2 - 3 - 4 - 1 - 2 - 3 - 4 -

Strawberry Roan

Count: 1 - 2 - 3 - 4 -

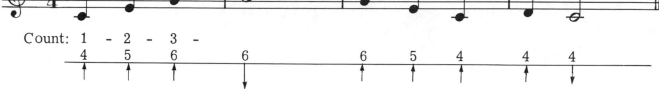

Count: 1 - 2 - 3 -

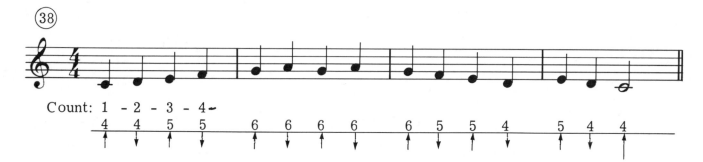

Count: 1 - 2 - 3 - 4 -

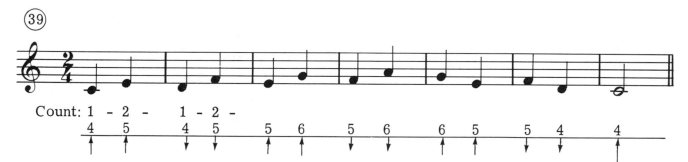

Count: 1 - 2 - 1 - 2 -

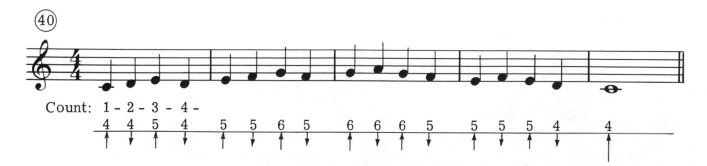

Count: 1 - 2 - 3 - 4 -

ALWAYS TAP YOUR FOOT!

Sanctus

F. Schubert

* Slurs: Two different notes to be played with one breath or played legato; not to
  be confused with tied notes of the same pitch.

Beautiful Brown Eyes

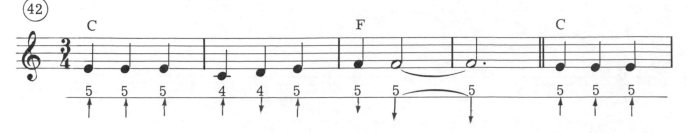

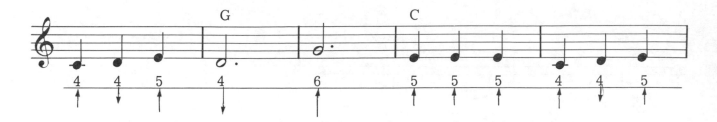

Look Down that Lonesome Road

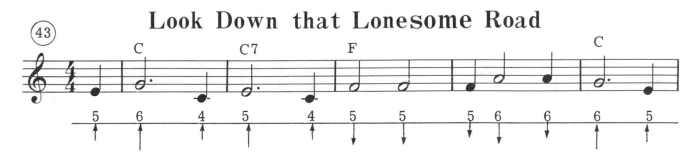

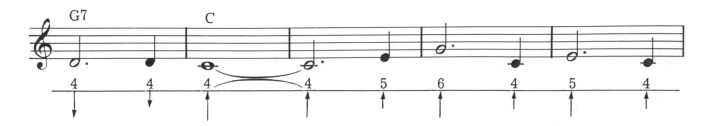

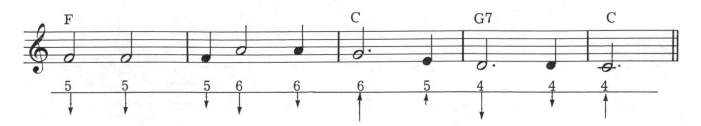

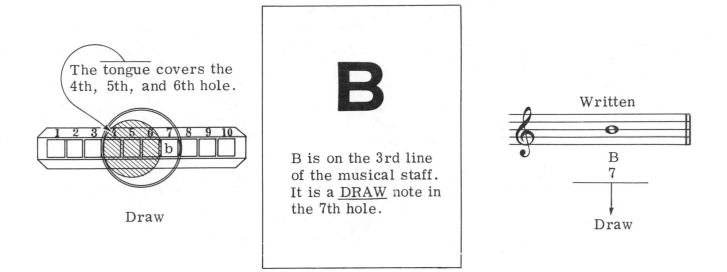

The tongue covers the 4th, 5th, and 6th hole.

Draw

B

B is on the 3rd line of the musical staff. It is a <u>DRAW</u> note in the 7th hole.

Written

B
7

Draw

Important:

Hole 4   Hole 5   Hole 6

Until now the pattern has been: Blow-Draw, Blow-Draw, Blow-Draw.

Hole 7

At the 7th hole this pattern is reversed; Draw-Blow.

(Reversed)

Hole 4	Hole 5	Hole 6	Hole 7
Blow-Draw	Blow-Draw	Blow-Draw	Draw-Blow
C d	E f	G a	b C

Example:

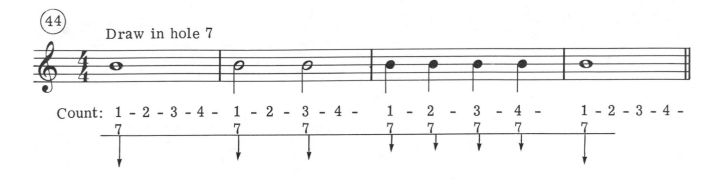

(44) Draw in hole 7

Count: 1 - 2 - 3 - 4 -   1 - 2 - 3 - 4 -   1 - 2 - 3 - 4 -   1 - 2 - 3 - 4 -

Long, Long Ago

Chapter IV

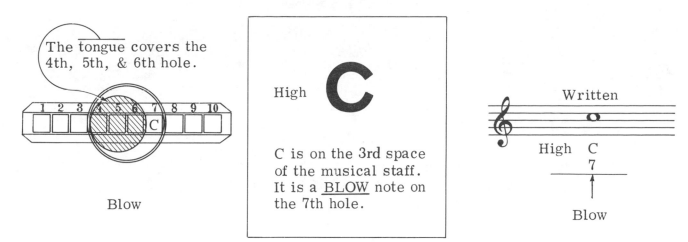

The tongue covers the 4th, 5th, & 6th hole.

Blow

High **C**

C is on the 3rd space of the musical staff. It is a <u>BLOW</u> note on the 7th hole.

Written

High C
7
Blow

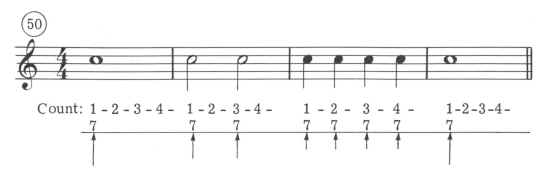

(50)

Count: 1 - 2 - 3 - 4 -   1 - 2 - 3 - 4 -   1 - 2 - 3 - 4 -   1-2-3-4-
7   7   7   7   7   7   7   7

"C" Scale

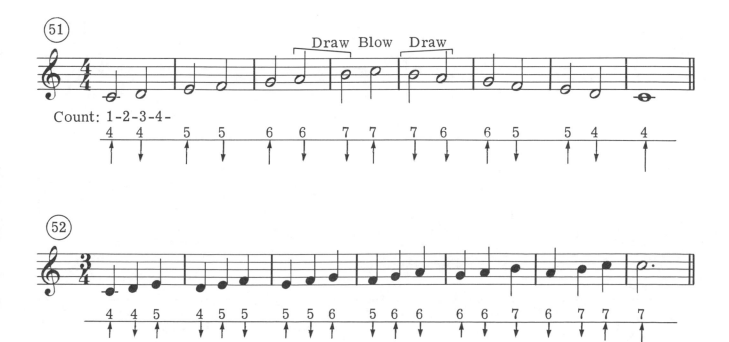

(51)

Draw   Blow   Draw

Count: 1-2-3-4-
4 4   5 5   6 6   7 7   7 6   6 5   5 4   4

(52)

4 4 5   4 5 5   5 5 6   5 6 6   6 6 7   6 7 7   7

Sweet Hour of Prayer

Little Annie Rooney

Billy Boy

31

The Marines' Hymn

Count: 3 - 4 -   1 - 2 - 3 - 4 -

How Can I Leave Thee

Drink to Me Only with Thine Eyes

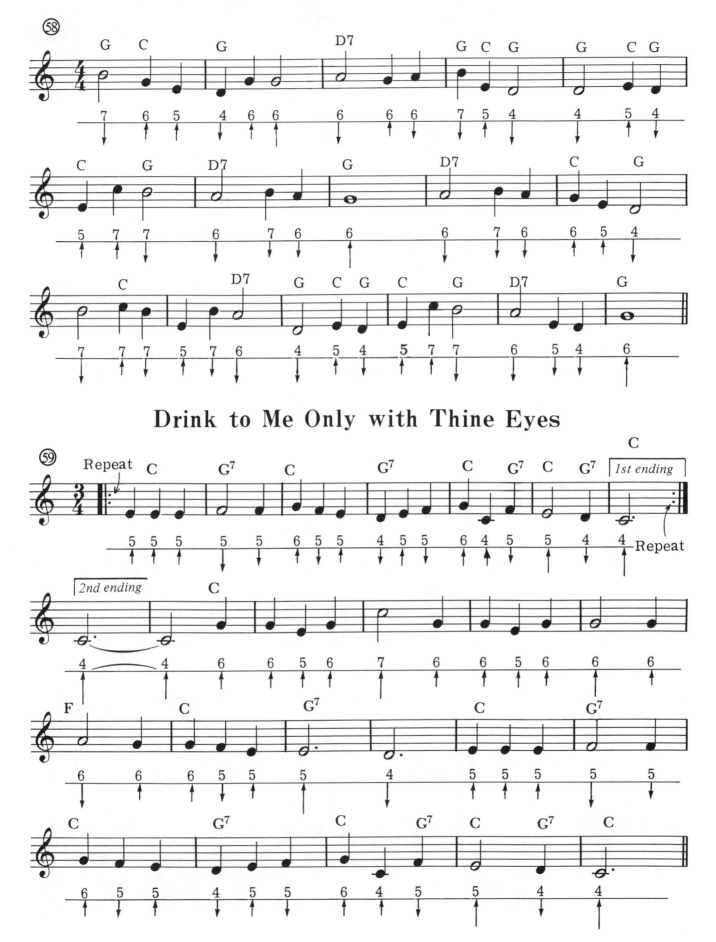

Eigth Note

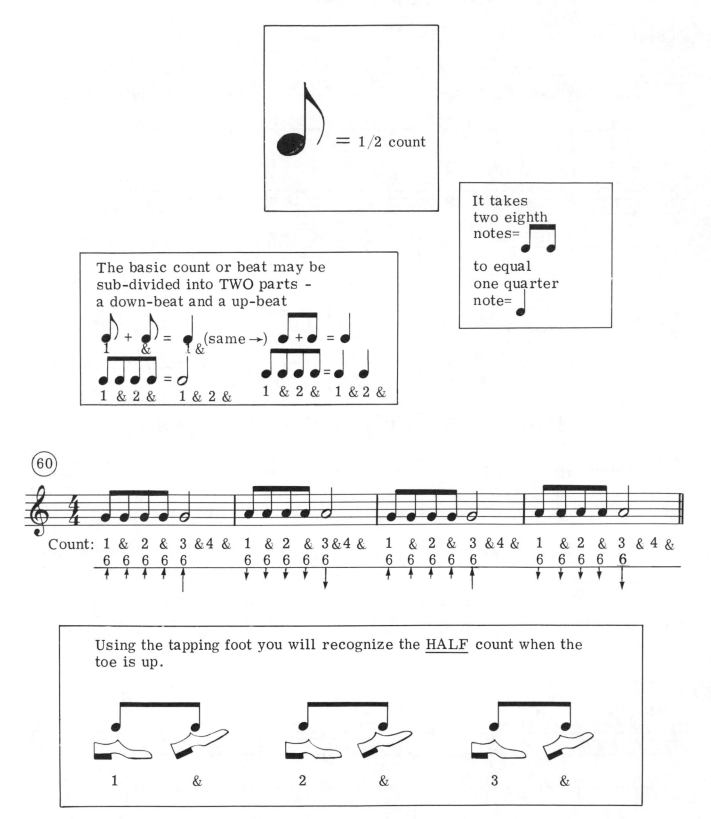

Minuet

J. S. Bach

Bach in Four

35

Alleluia

Blue Bells of Scotland

Sweet Betsy from Pike

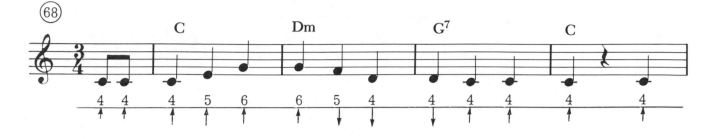

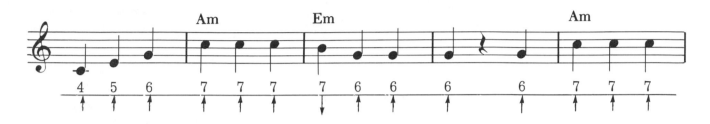

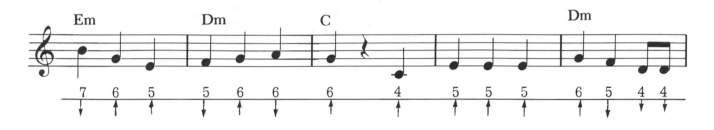

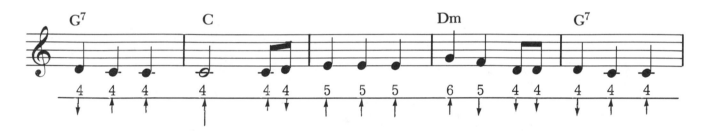

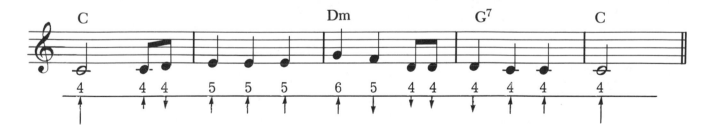

Chapter V

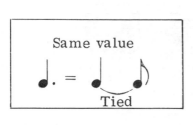

Same value

Tied

Dotted Quarter Note

$1\frac{1}{2}$ counts

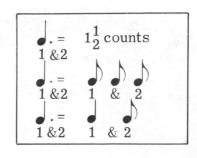

70

Count: 1 & 2 & 3 &   1 & 2 & 3 &   1 & 2 & 3 &   1 & 2 & 3 &   1 & 2 & 3 &

Schubert's Waltz

71

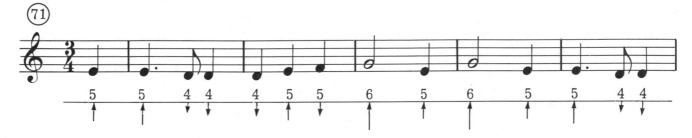

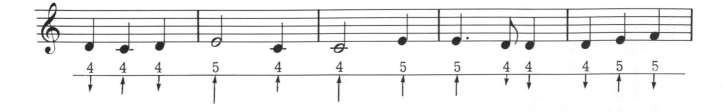

She Wore a Yellow Ribbon

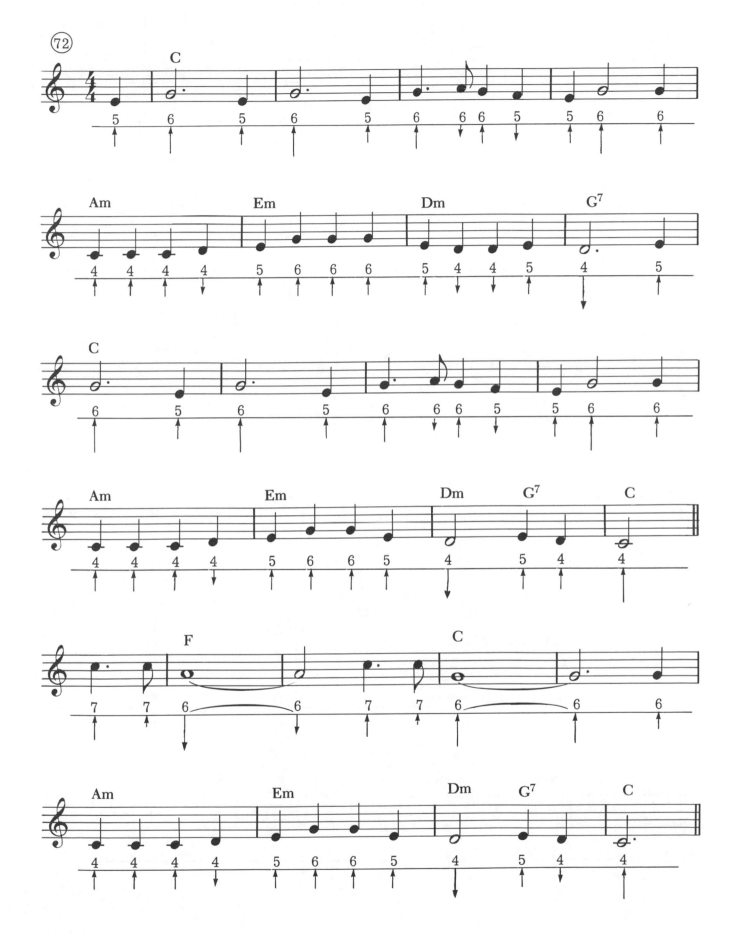

Whispering Hope

Alice Hawthorne

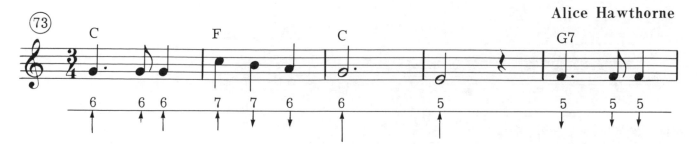

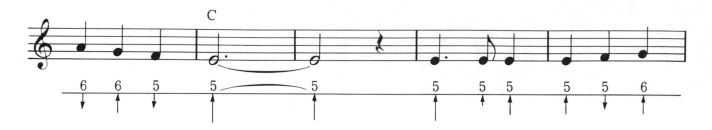

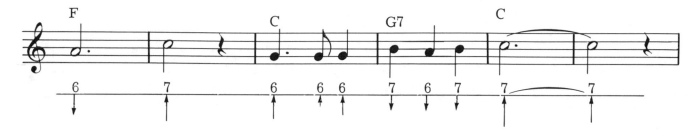

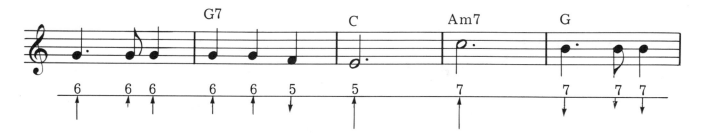

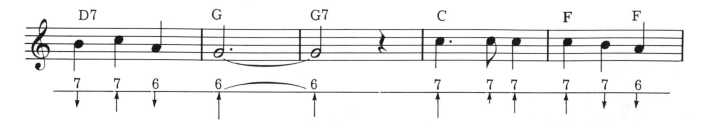

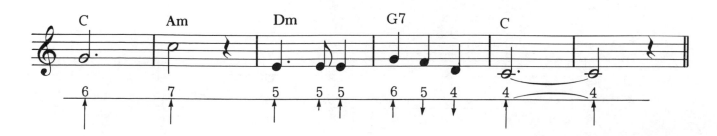

Joy to the World

G. F. Handel

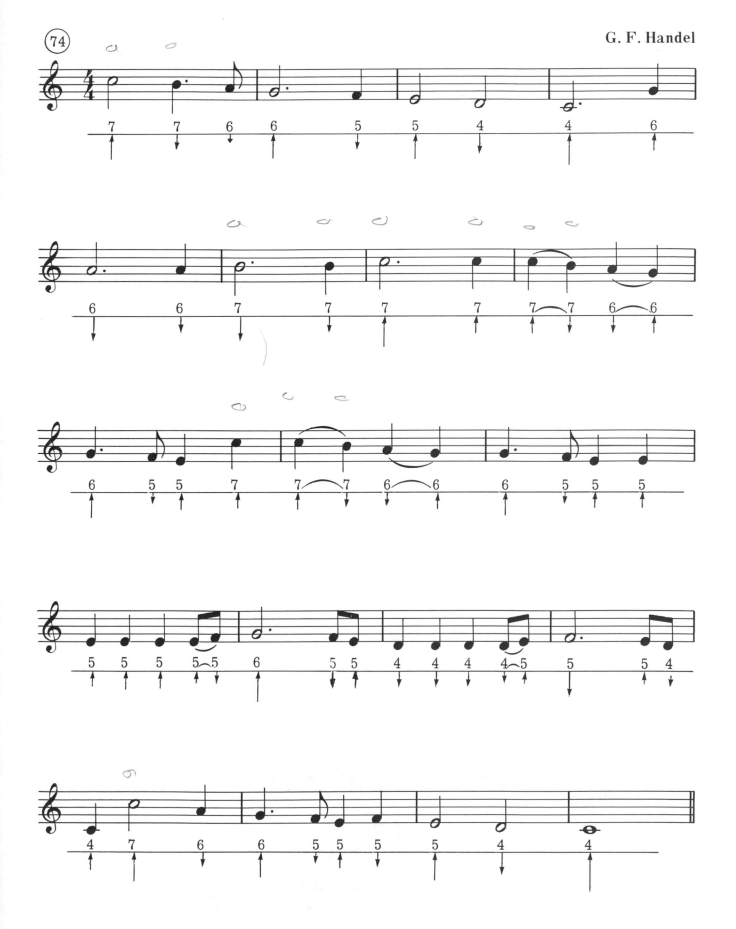

French Folk Tune

Complete Silence

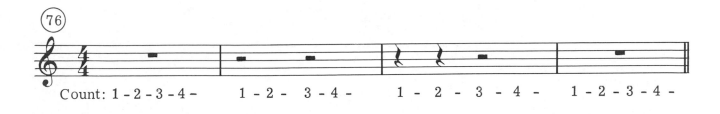

Resting in Three

Strange Places

Chapter VI

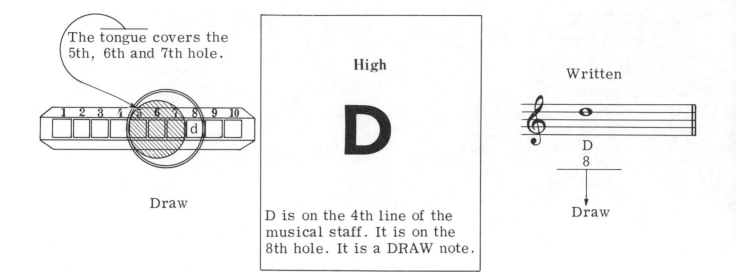

The tongue covers the 5th, 6th and 7th hole.

Draw

High

D

D is on the 4th line of the musical staff. It is on the 8th hole. It is a DRAW note.

Written

D
8

Draw

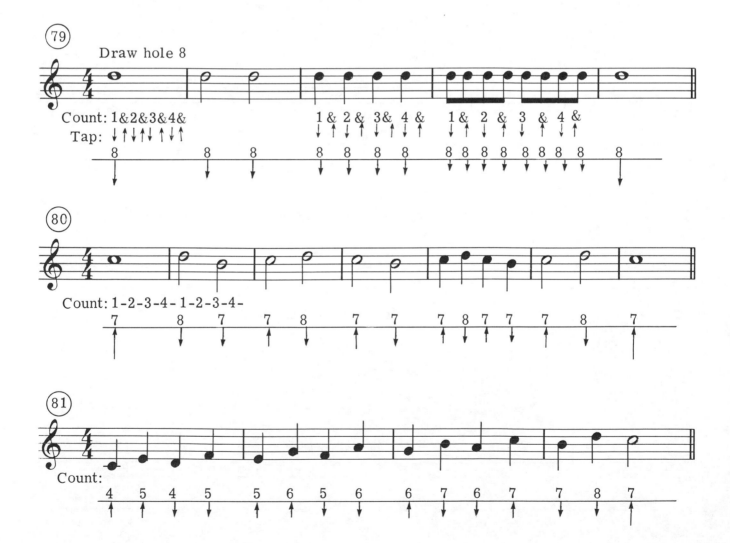

Country Gardens

Peer Gynt Suite

Beethoven

Duet

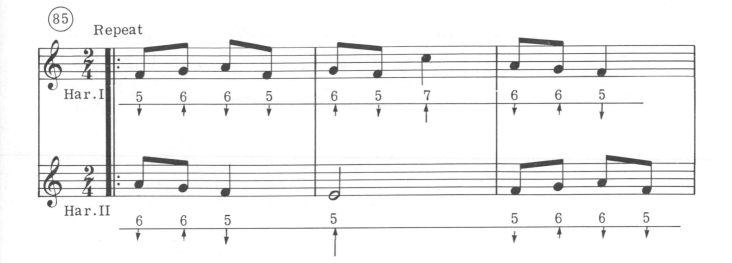

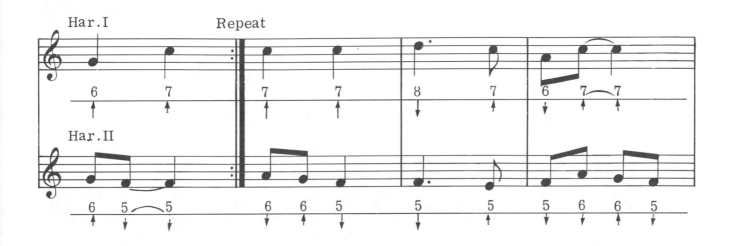

Cowboy

Nobody Knows the Trouble I've Seen

Swanee River

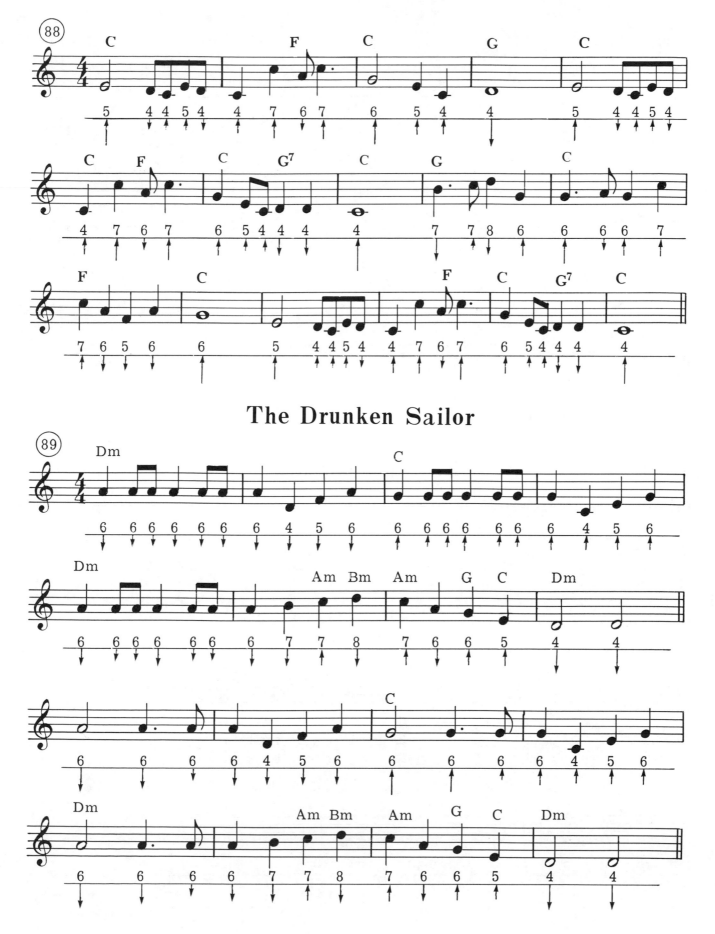

The Drunken Sailor

Humoreske

Dvorak

Old Netherlands

Folk Song

While Shepherds Watched

G. F. Handel

I Gave My Love a Cherry

The Caisson Song

Count: 3 & 4 &

Eighth Rest

2 Eighth rests equal one quarter rest

$\gamma = \frac{1}{2}$ count

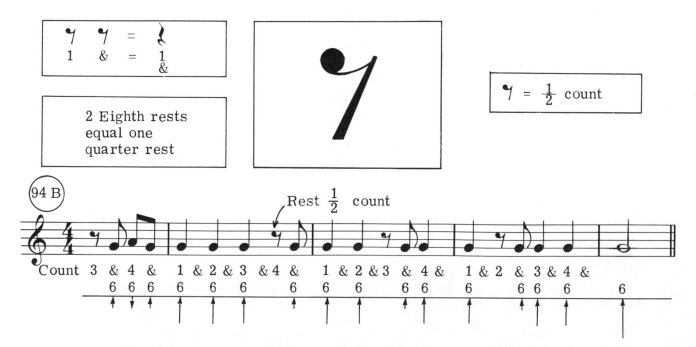

Rest $\frac{1}{2}$ count

Count 3 & 4 &

Chapter VII

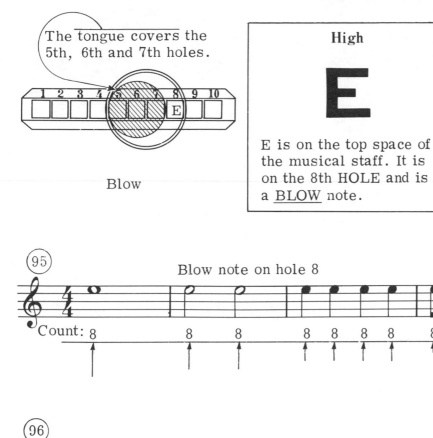

The tongue covers the 5th, 6th and 7th holes.

Blow

High

E

E is on the top space of the musical staff. It is on the 8th HOLE and is a **BLOW** note.

Written

E
8

Blow

(95) Blow note on hole 8

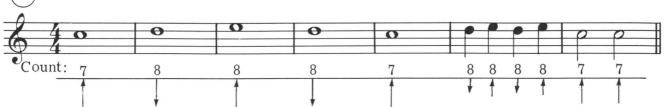

Count: 8   8   8   8 8 8 8   8 8 8 8 8 8 8 8   8

(96)

Count: 7   8   8   8   7   8 8 8 8   7   7

(97)

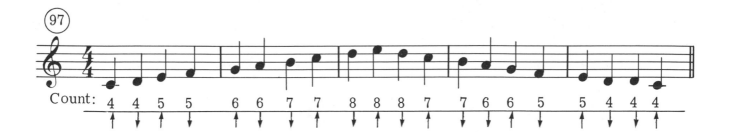

Count: 4 4 5 5   6 6 7 7   8 8 8 7   7 6 6 5   5 4 4 4

(98)

Count: 4 4 5 5   4 5 5 6   5 5 6 6   5 6 6 7   6 6 7 7   6 7 7 8   7 7 8 8   7

Largo

A. Dvorak

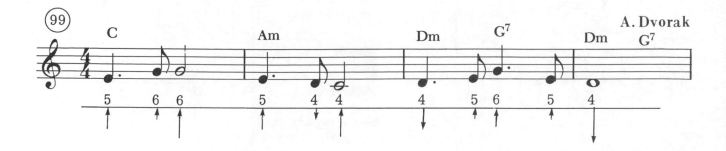

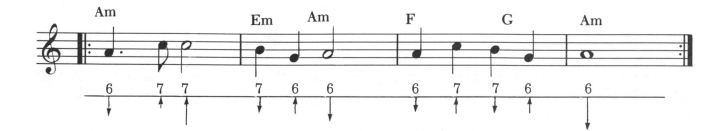

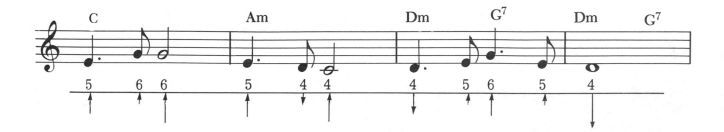

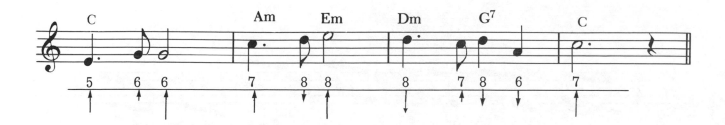

Schumann Op. 68, No. 19

Old Time Religion

Worried Man Blues

Annie Laurie

Little Brown Jug

My Wild Irish Rose

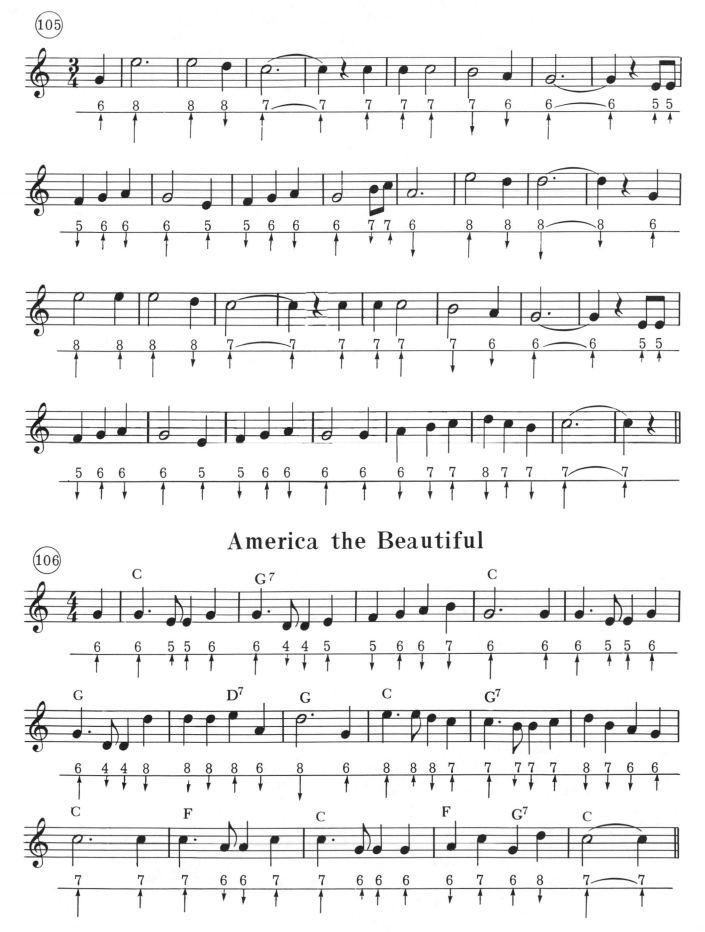

America the Beautiful

Our Boys Will Shine Tonight

Wildwood Flower

Dixie

Chapter VIII

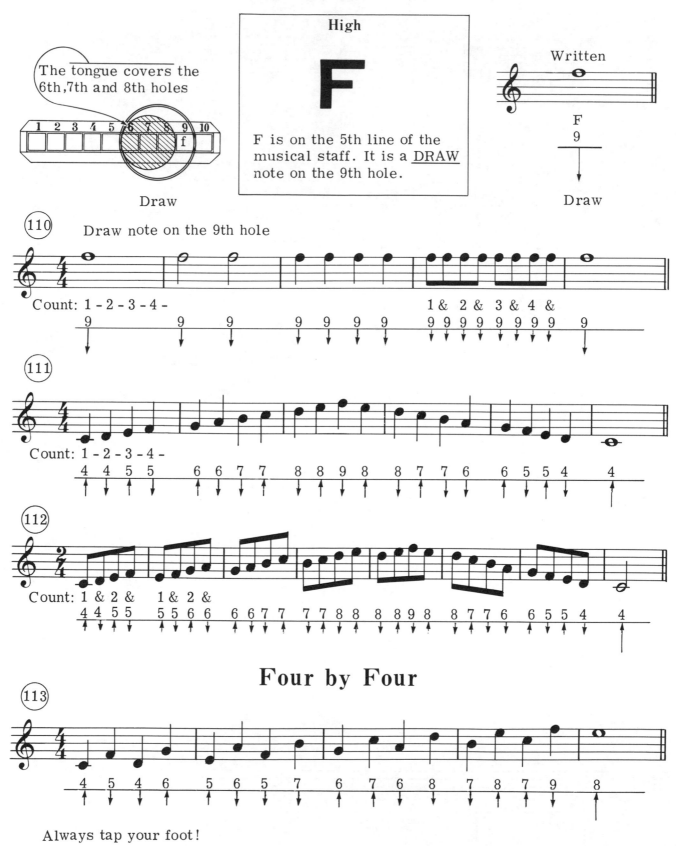

The tongue covers the 6th, 7th and 8th holes

Draw

High F

F is on the 5th line of the musical staff. It is a <u>DRAW</u> note on the 9th hole.

Written

F
9

Draw

Four by Four

Always tap your foot!

Alma Mater

Cielito Lindo

Johannes Brahms Op. 39, No. 2

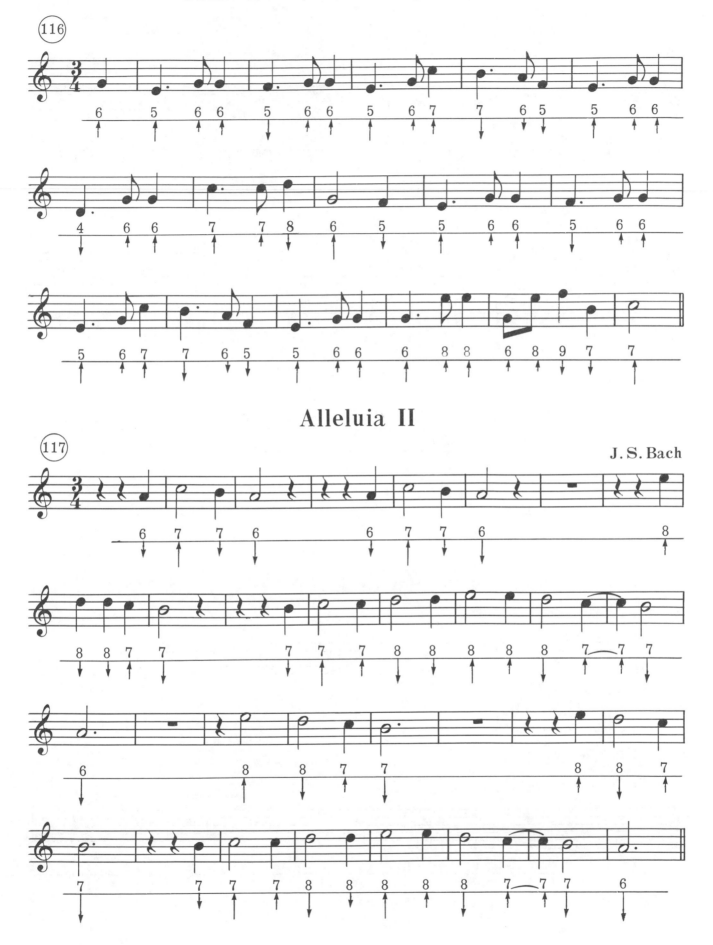

Alleluia II

J. S. Bach

63

We Wish You a Merry Christmas

Swan Lake

Aura Lee

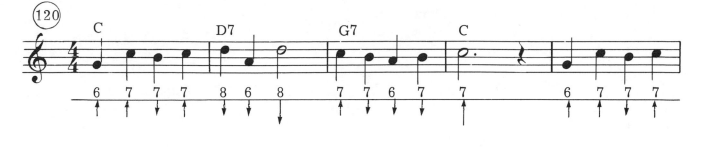

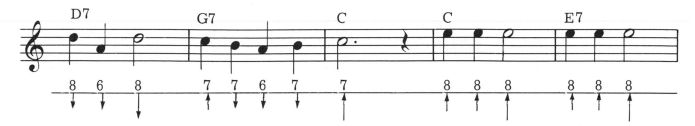

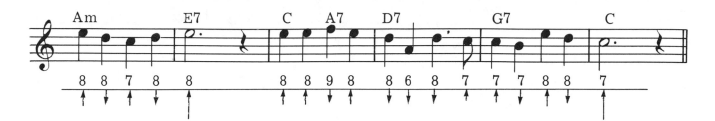

The Yellow Rose of Texas

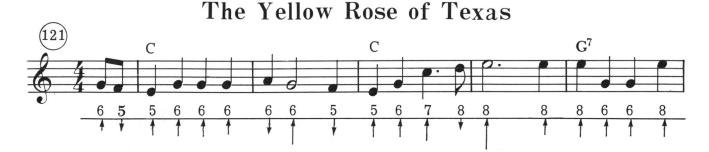

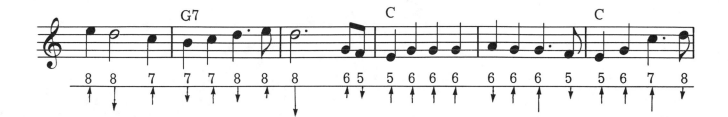

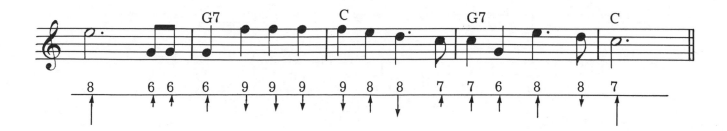

Chapter IX

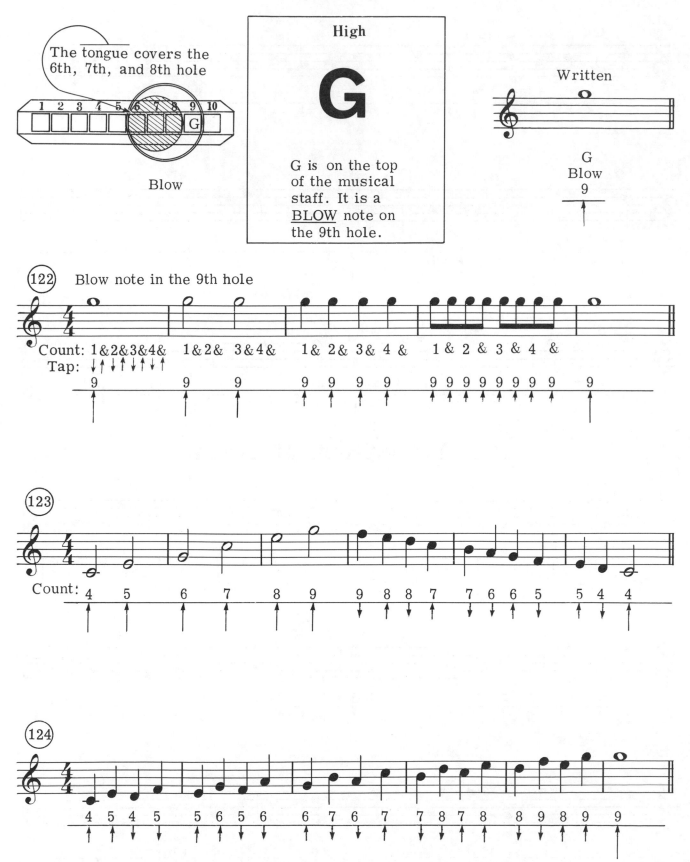

The tongue covers the 6th, 7th, and 8th hole

Blow

High

G

G is on the top of the musical staff. It is a **BLOW** note on the 9th hole.

Written

G
Blow
9

(122) Blow note in the 9th hole

Count: 1 & 2 & 3 & 4 &   1 & 2 &   3 & 4 &   1 & 2 & 3 & 4 &   1 & 2 & 3 & 4 &
Tap: ↓ ↑ ↓ ↑ ↓ ↑ ↓ ↑
9   9   9   9 9 9 9   9 9 9 9 9 9 9 9   9

(123)

Count: 4   5   6   7   8   9   9   8   8   7   7   6   6   5   5   4   4

(124)

4 5 4 5   5 6 5 6   6 7 6 7   7 8 7 8   8 9 8 9   9

66

Home on the Range

Sonata

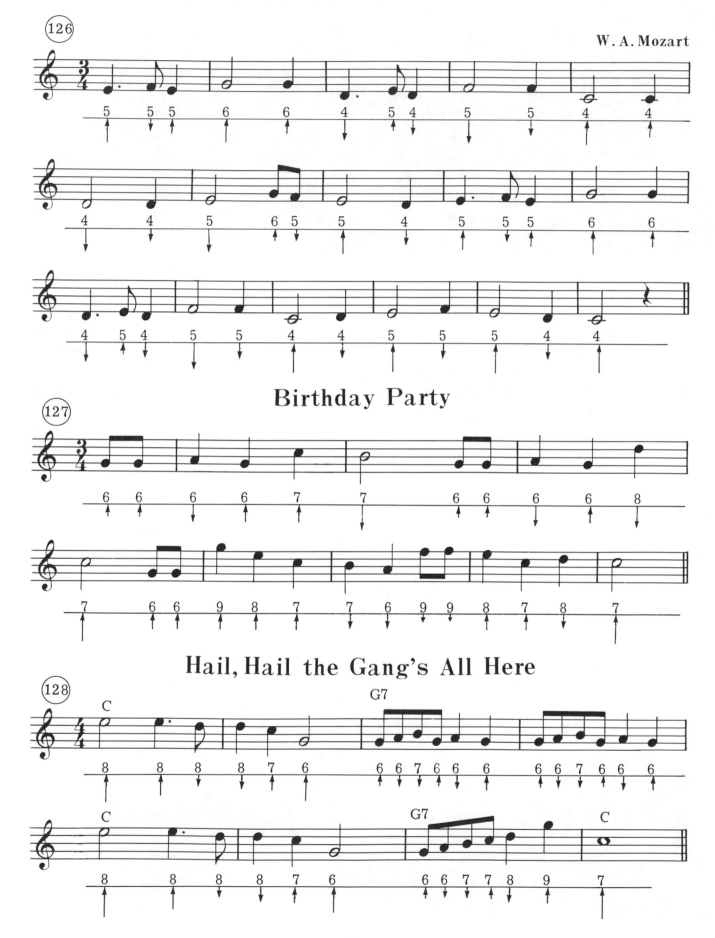

Birthday Party

Hail, Hail the Gang's All Here

Pathetique

P. I. Tchaikovsky

Red River Valley

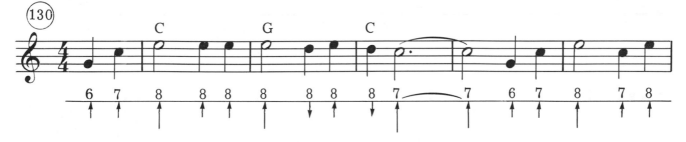

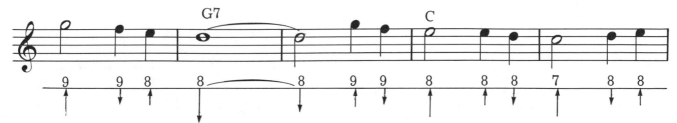

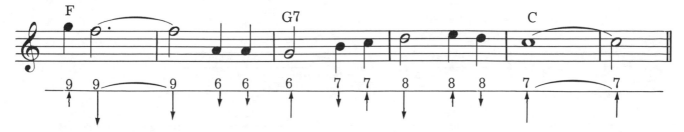

The Triplet

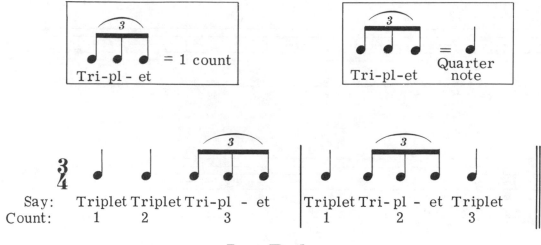

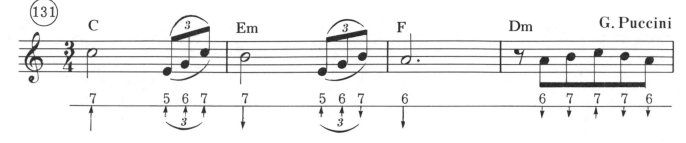

Say: Triplet Triplet Tri-pl - et | Triplet Tri-pl - et Triplet
Count: 1 2 3 | 1 2 3

La Boheme

G. Puccini

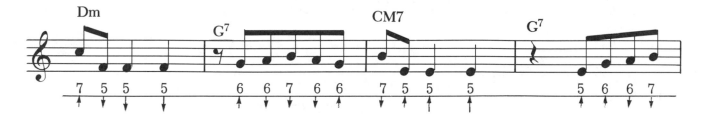

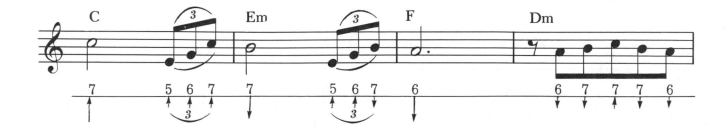

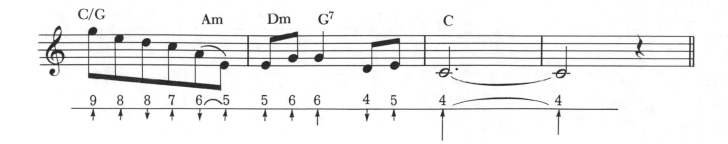

Examination

1. A music staff is composed of _____ lines and _____ spaces.

2. Name the lines. _____

3. Name the spaces. _____

4. The top number in a time signature tells the _____ of counts

   in a _____ .

5. The lower number in a time signature tells the kind of a note

   that gets _____ count.

6. In $\frac{4}{4}$ time a whole note (𝅝) gets _____ counts.

7. In $\frac{3}{4}$ time a half note (𝅗𝅥) gets _____ counts.

8. The musical alphabet is composed of _____ letters. They

   are _____ .

9. When a piece begins with an incomplete measure, we find the

   remainder of the count in the _____ measure.

10. Rests are signs of _____ .

11. When two notes are tied (𝅗𝅥 𝅗𝅥) should the second note be repeated?

    _____ .

12. Change the following notes to quarter notes.

13. When three note are placed together , they are

    called _____ .

Chapter X

The tongue covers the 7th, 8th, and 9th holes.

Draw

High

A

A is on the first leger line above the musical staff. It is a DRAW note in the 10th hole.

Written

A
10

Draw

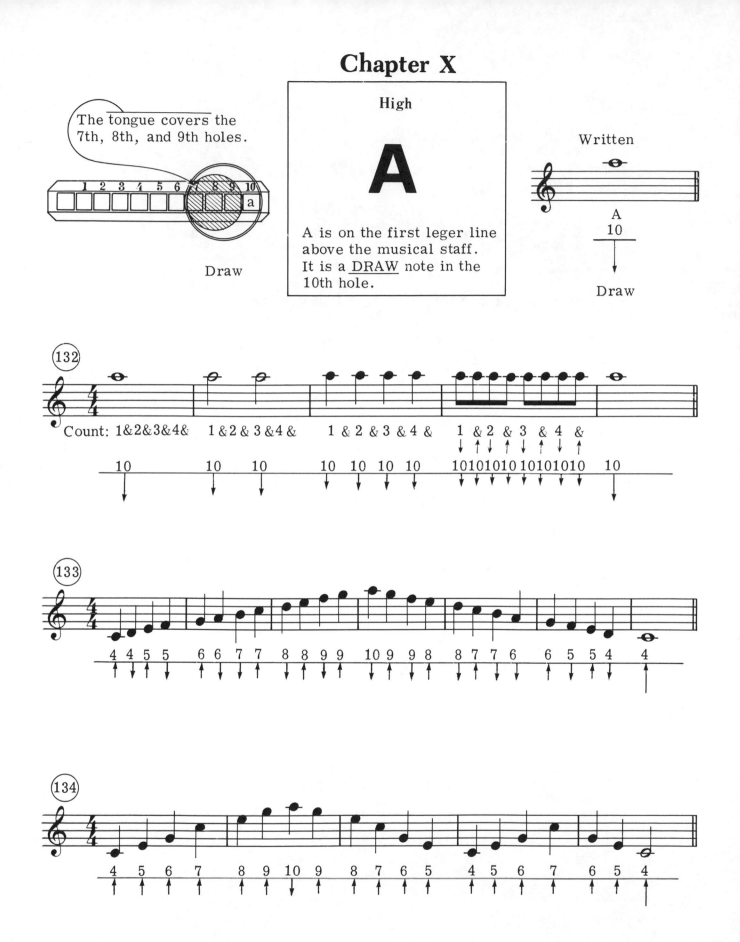

72

God Rest Ye Merry, Gentleman

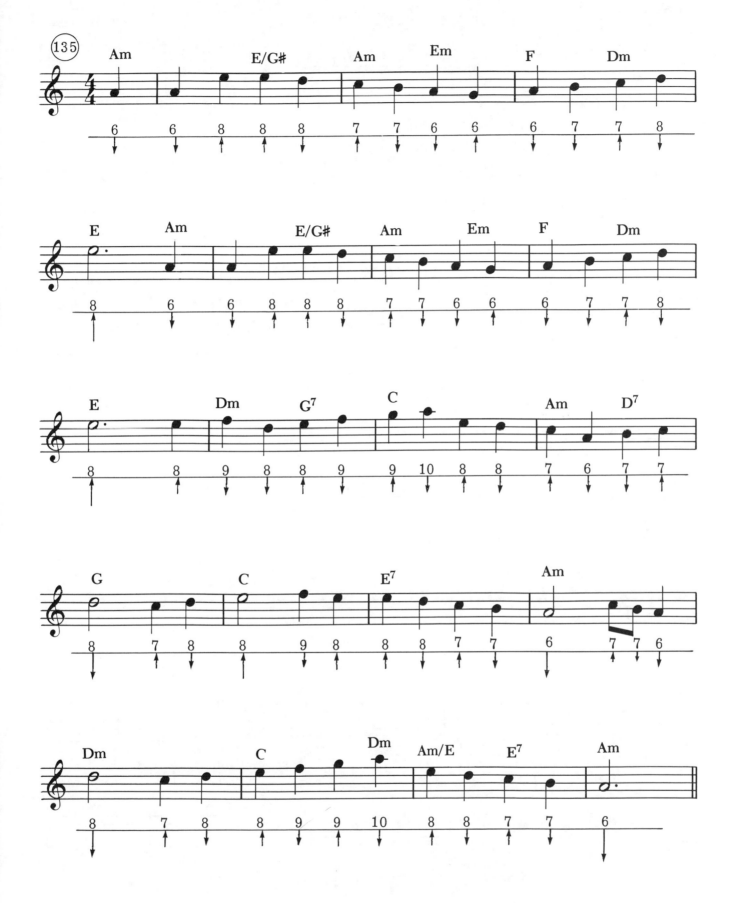

Nearer, My God, to Thee

Lowell Mason

Old Hundredth(1551)

Bourgeios

All Through the Night

Silent Night

America *

Looby Lou *

°Could be played one octave
lower, hole 4, 5 & 6.

Chapter XI

On the "C" harmonica there is no "B" note on the upper register.

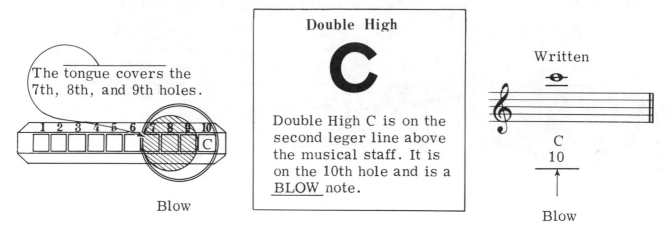

The tongue covers the 7th, 8th, and 9th holes.

Blow

Double High

C

Double High C is on the second leger line above the musical staff. It is on the 10th hole and is a BLOW note.

Written

C
10

Blow

$\frac{4}{4}$ is the most "Common" time signature. Some times a "C" is used to express $\frac{4}{4}$ time.

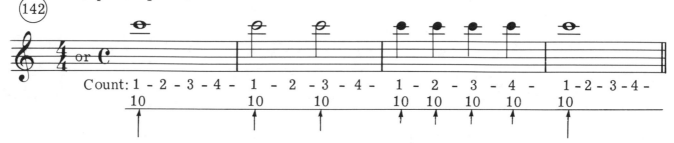

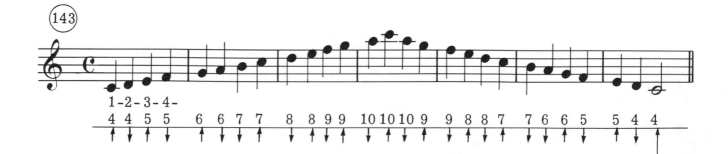

Battle Hymn of the Republic

Cut time
(Twice as fast
as written)

William Steffe

"C" Harmonica

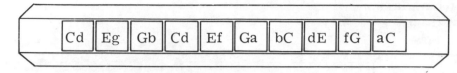

Large letters: Blow notes
Small letters: Draw notes

Turkey in the Straw

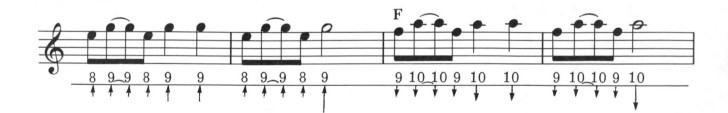

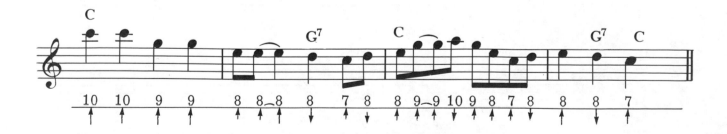

Chapter XII

The tongue covers the 1st and 2nd holes.

Draw

Low B

Low B is below the first leger line below the musical staff. It is on the 3rd hole and is a DRAW note.

Written

B
3

Draw

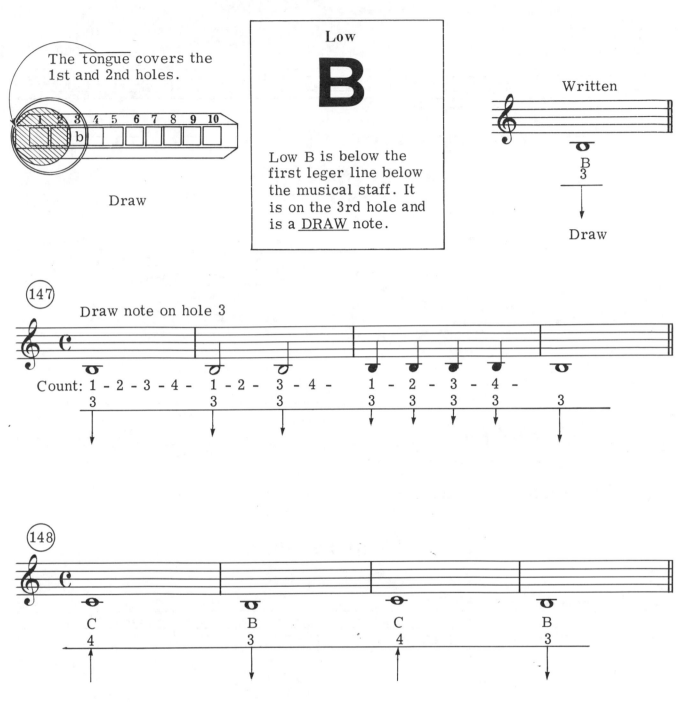

(147) Draw note on hole 3

Count: 1 - 2 - 3 - 4 -   1 - 2 - 3 - 4 -   1 - 2 - 3 - 4 -   3
3   3   3   3   3   3   3   3

(148)

C   B   C   B
4   3   4   3

(149)

4 4 4   4 3 4   4 5 4   4 3 4

79

Mozart Sonata in C

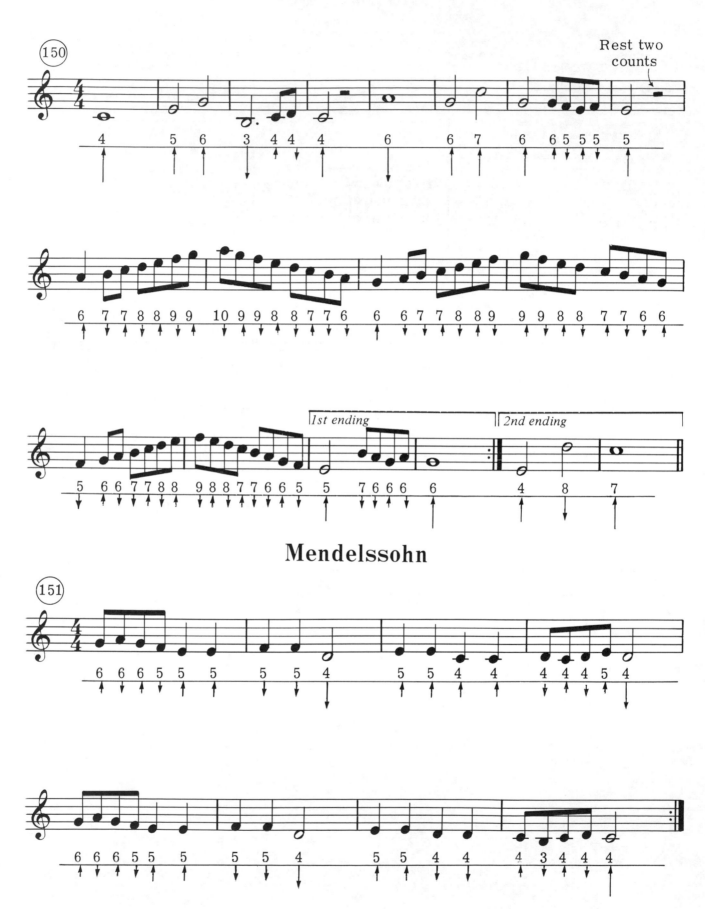

Mendelssohn

La Spagnola

Mary Ann

D.C. (To the beginning) al (Then go to) Finc (Finish)

81

Jesu, Joy of Man's Desiring

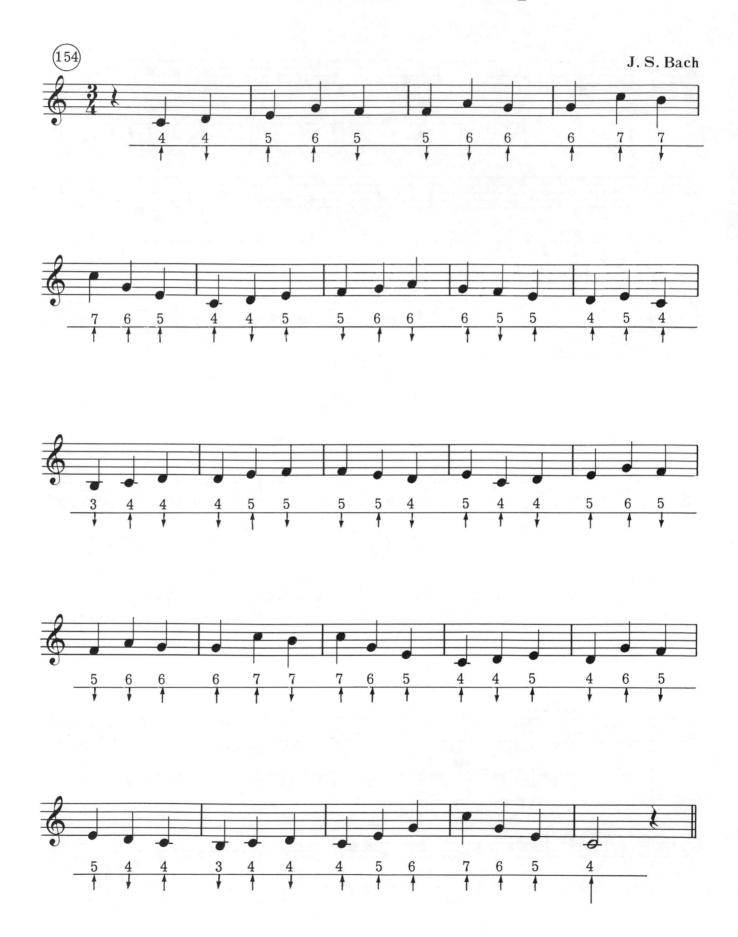

J. S. Bach

Chapter XIII

The tongue covers hole one and two.

Blow

Low G

G is below the musical staff, below 2 leger lines. It is a **BLOW** note in the 3rd hole of the harmonica.

Written

Second leger line

G
Blow
3

(155) There is no "A" note in the lower register of the harmonica

Count: 1 & 2 & 3 & 4 &

1 & 2 & 3 & 4 &
Tap foot

(156)

Buffalo Gals

(157)

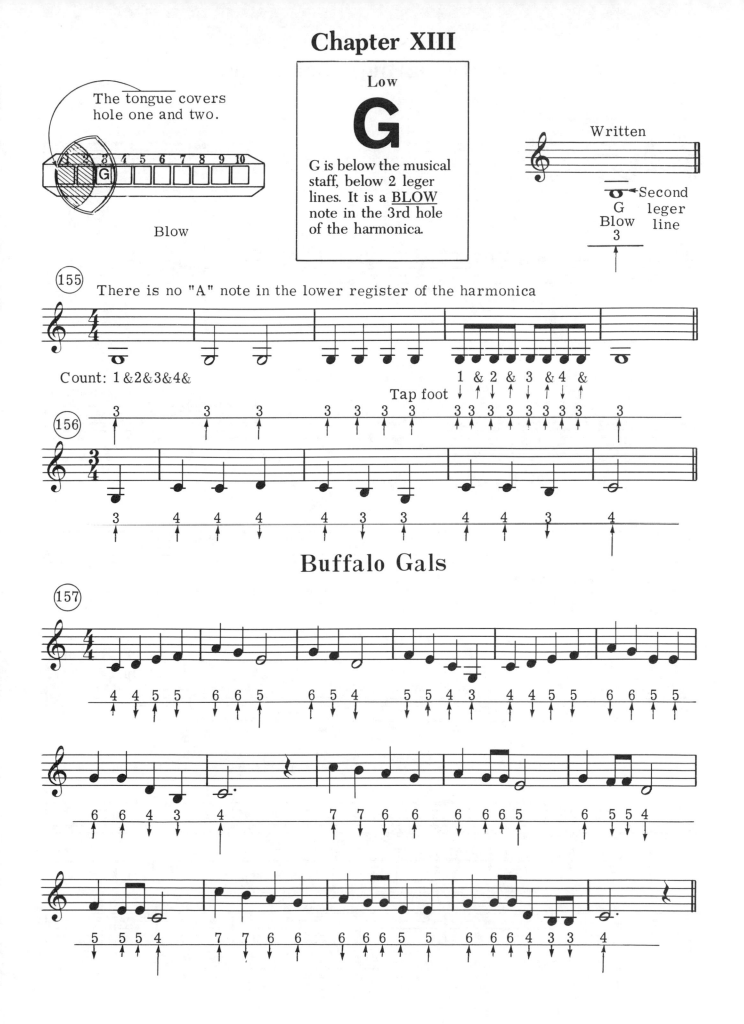

Oh, My Darling Clementine

William Tell

Rossini

Impromptu

F. Schubert
Op. 142, No. 2

Down in the Valley

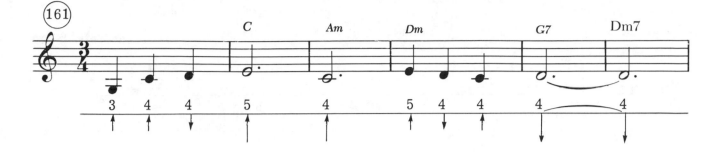

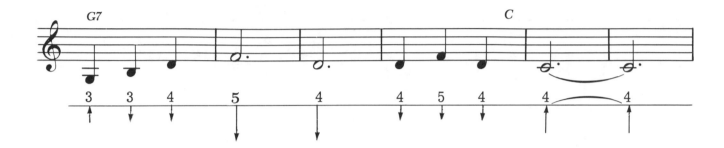

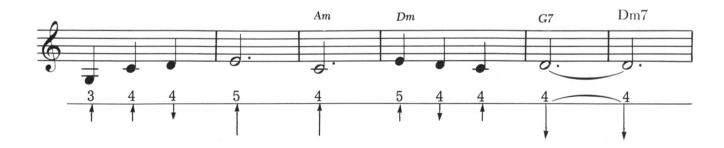

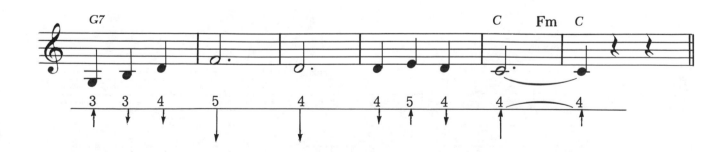

Chapanecas

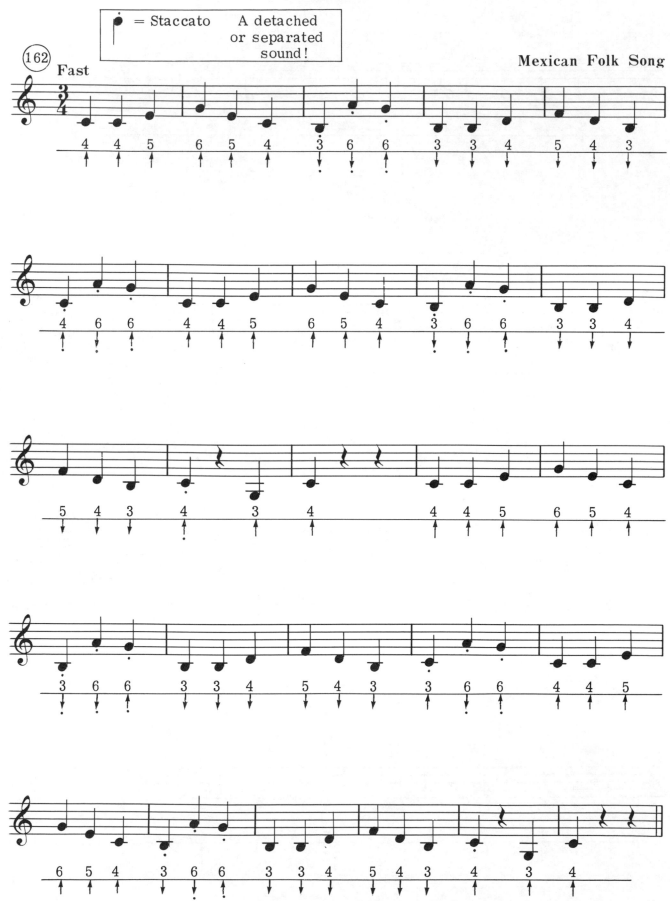

Alouette

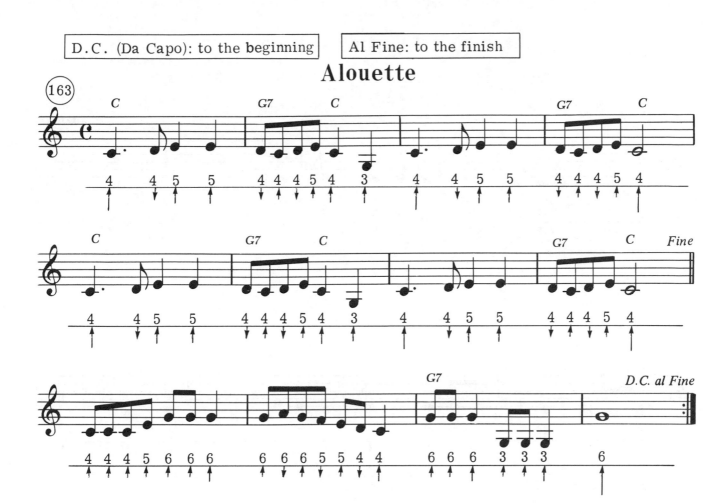

Careless Love

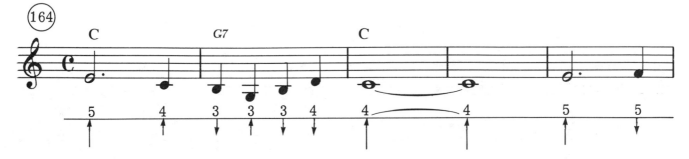

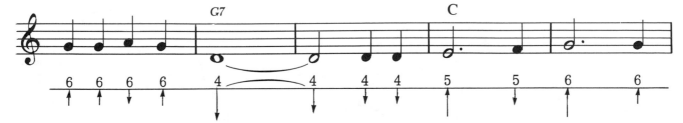

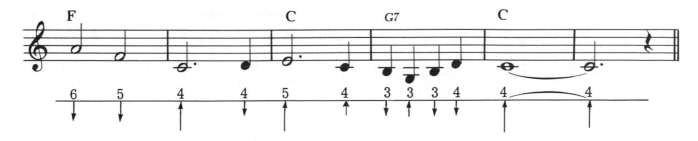

O Christmas Tree

German

Bridal Chorus

Boogie Woogie

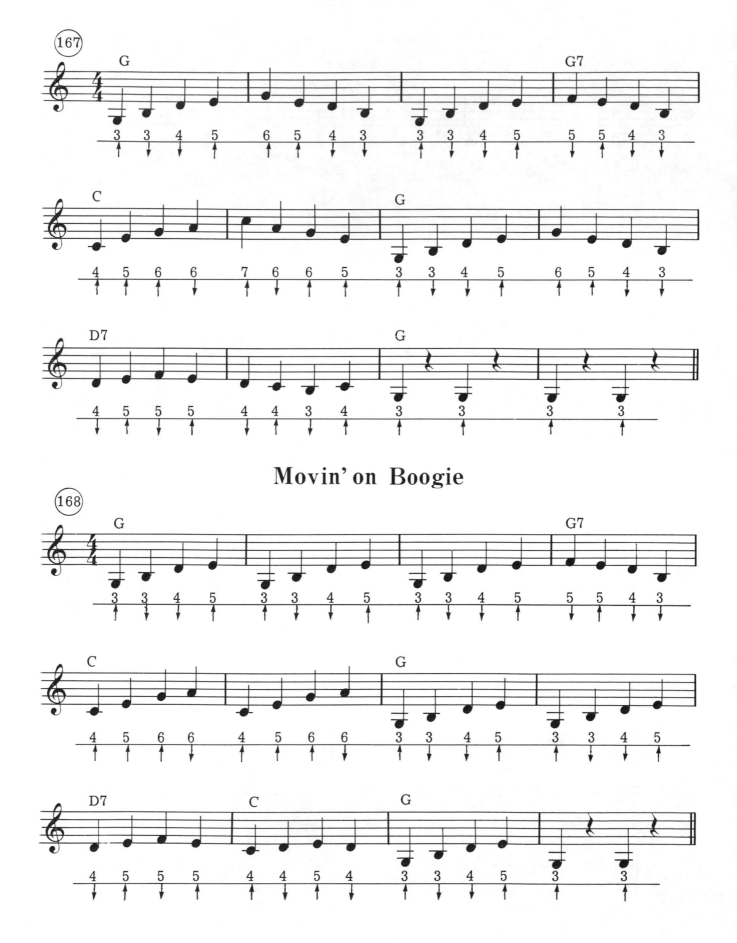

Movin' on Boogie

Bounce Boogie

Stroll Boogie

Chapter XIV

When Johnny Comes Marching Home

House of the Rising Sun

Funny Times

Dance in Six — Eight

When the Dot is above or below the note it is a staccato. (A detached or separated sound)

I Saw Three Ships

Auprés de Ma Blonde

Jig

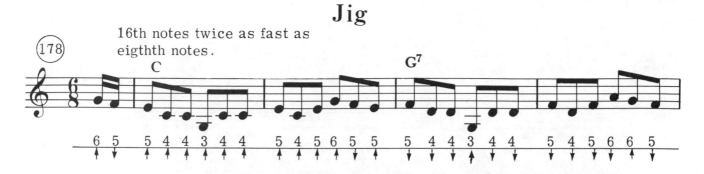

Moldau

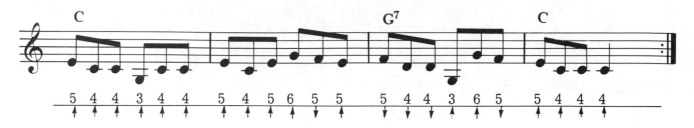

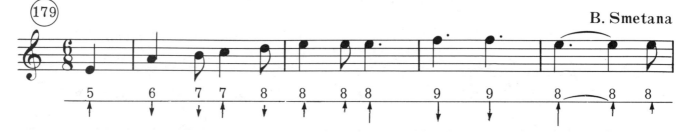

Harvest Song

Here We Come A – Wassailing

Old English

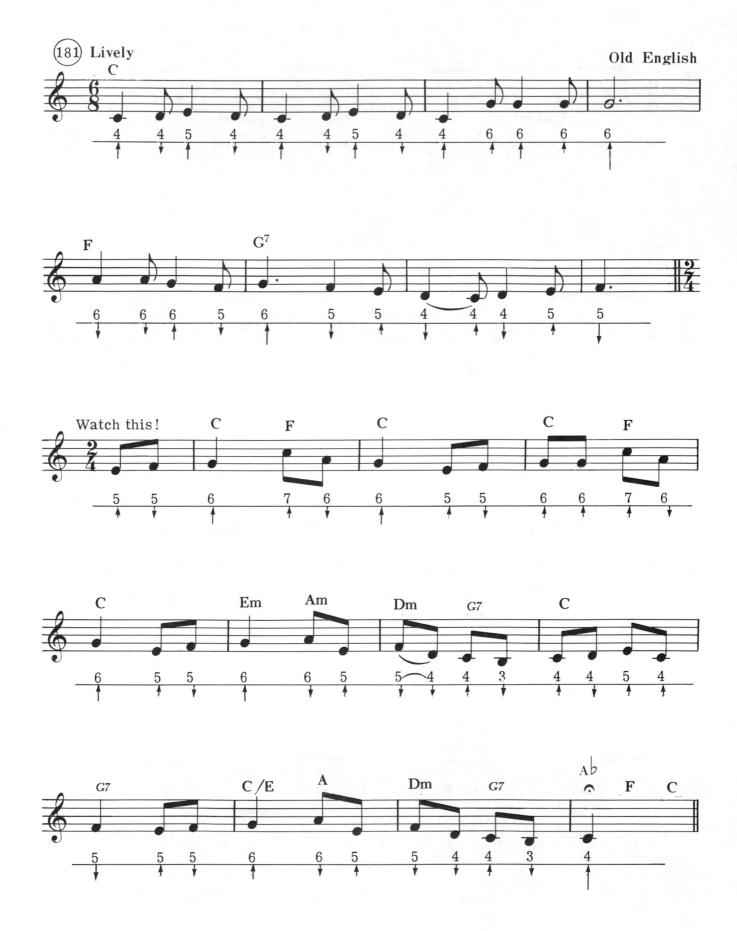

Chapter XV

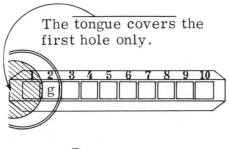

The tongue covers the
first hole only.

Draw

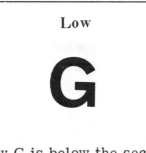

Low

G

Low G is below the second
leger line below the staff.
It is on the 2nd hole. It
is a <u>DRAW</u> note.

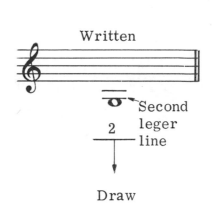

Written

Second
leger
line

Draw

This note is usually used for <u>Blues</u>. Drawing the G note (in hole 2) as

opposed the blowing the G note (in hole 3) allows blues players to use

a"blues"technique called bending. However, it originally was used for

the "G" chord (three notes played together). When drawing in holes

2, 3, and 4 you get the notes G-B-D. <u>That is the G chord.</u>

Example

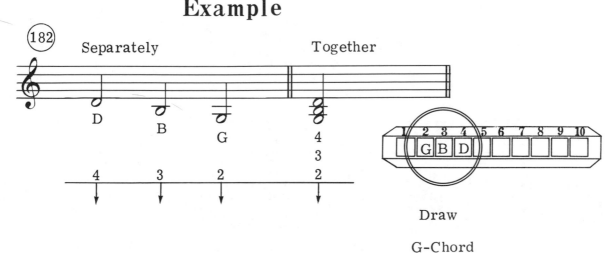

Draw

G-Chord

There is <u>no "F" note</u> in the lower register of the harmonica.

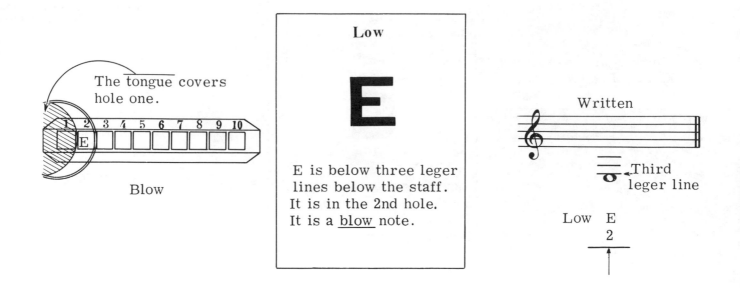

Low

E

E is below three leger lines below the staff. It is in the 2nd hole. It is a <u>blow</u> note.

Written

Third leger line

Low   E
2

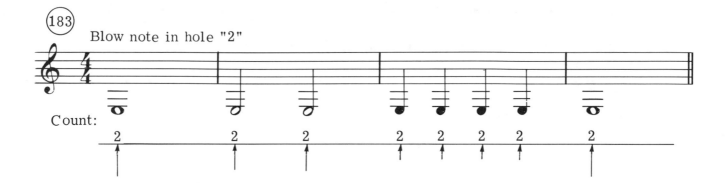

(183)   Blow note in hole "2"

Count: 2   2   2   2   2   2   2   2

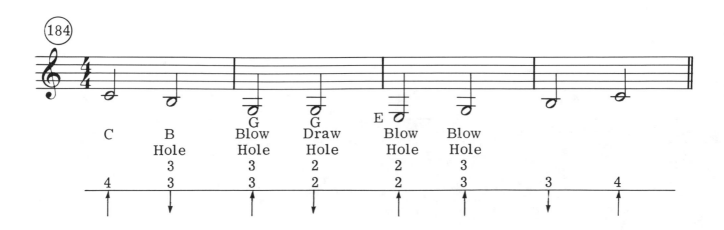

(184)

C   B   G   G   E   Blow
         Blow   Draw   Blow   Hole
Hole   Hole   Hole   Hole
3   3   2   2   3
4   3   3   2   2   3   3   4

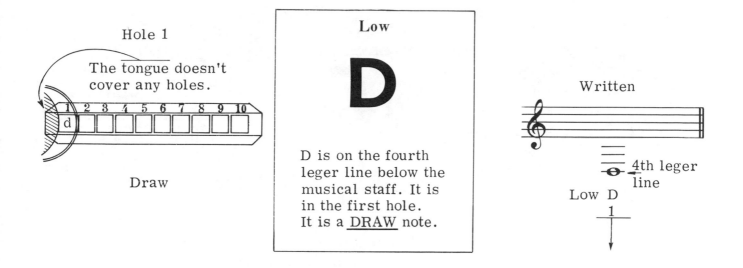

Hole 1

The tongue doesn't cover any holes.

Draw

Low

D

D is on the fourth leger line below the musical staff. It is in the first hole. It is a **DRAW** note.

Written

Low D 1

4th leger line

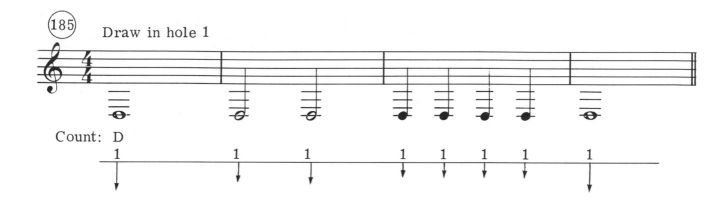

(185) Draw in hole 1

Count: D
1   1   1   1 1 1 1   1

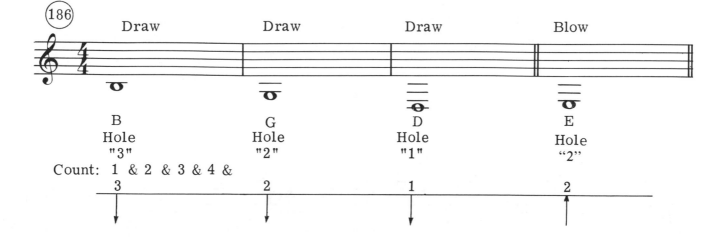

(186)

Draw   Draw   Draw   Blow

B   G   D   E
Hole   Hole   Hole   Hole
"3"   "2"   "1"   "2"

Count: 1 & 2 & 3 & 4 &
3   2   1   2

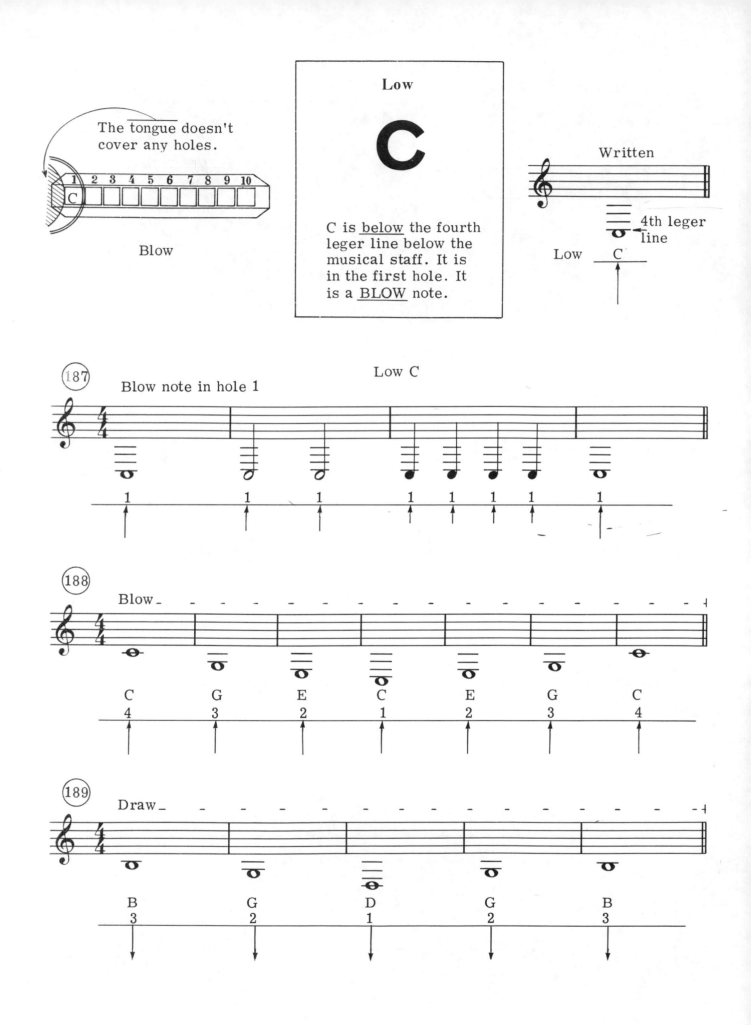

The tongue doesn't cover any holes.

Blow

Low

C

C is below the fourth leger line below the musical staff. It is in the first hole. It is a BLOW note.

Written

4th leger line

Low C

Low C

187 Blow note in hole 1

188 Blow

C 4   G 3   E 2   C 1   E 2   G 3   C 4

189 Draw

B 3   G 2   D 1   G 2   B 3

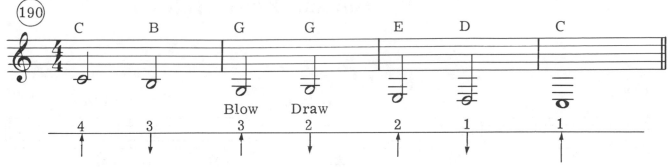

Now <u>BLOW</u> into the bottom 4 holes without the tongue.

Example

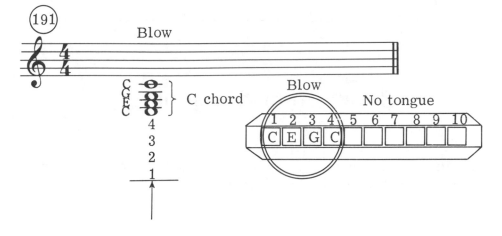

Now <u>DRAW</u> into the bottom 4 holes without the tongue.

Example

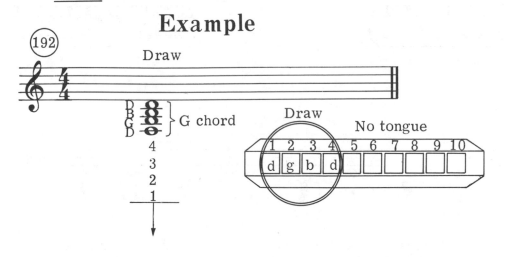

Bottom Four Holes

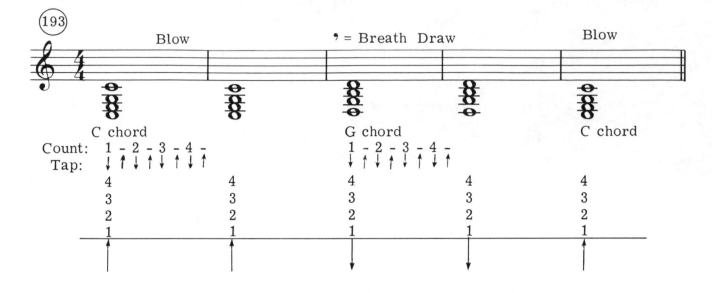

Blow — Note & Chord

Use the tongue to cover holes 1, 2, & 3. Leave hole four open. Now release the tongue on holes 1, 2, & 3. Repeat.

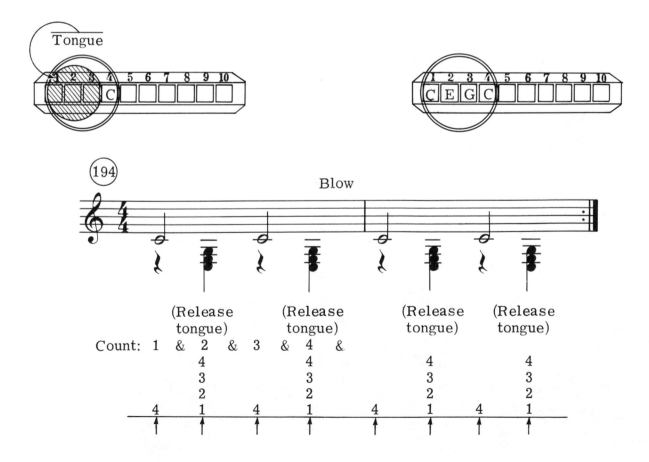

Draw – Note & Chord

Use the tongue to cover holes 1, 2, & 3. Leave hole 4 open. Now release the tongue on hole 1, 2, & 3. Repeat.

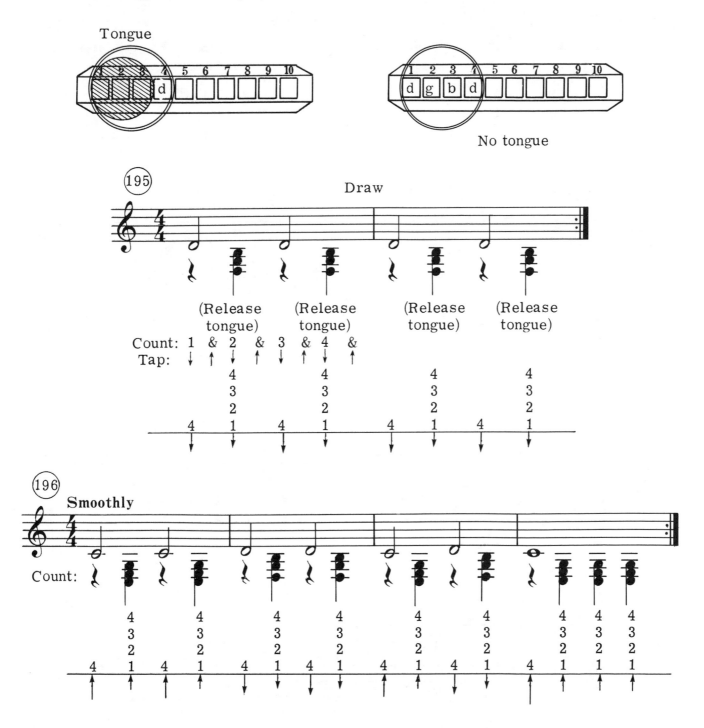

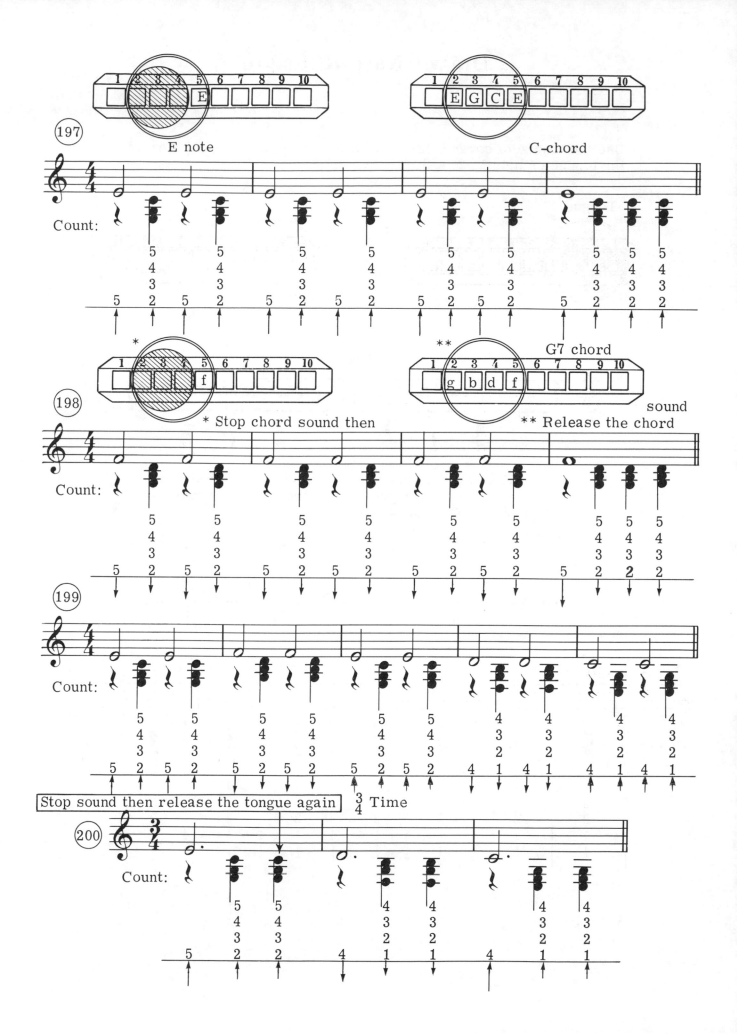

Hot Cross Buns

Mary's Lamb

Quick release of the tongue, then back in position with the tongue.

107

The following are excerpts from different songs. Four or more measures of examples of how to insert chords in different melodies. Examine the following then go back to your favorite tunes and interject these chords to suit your pleasure.

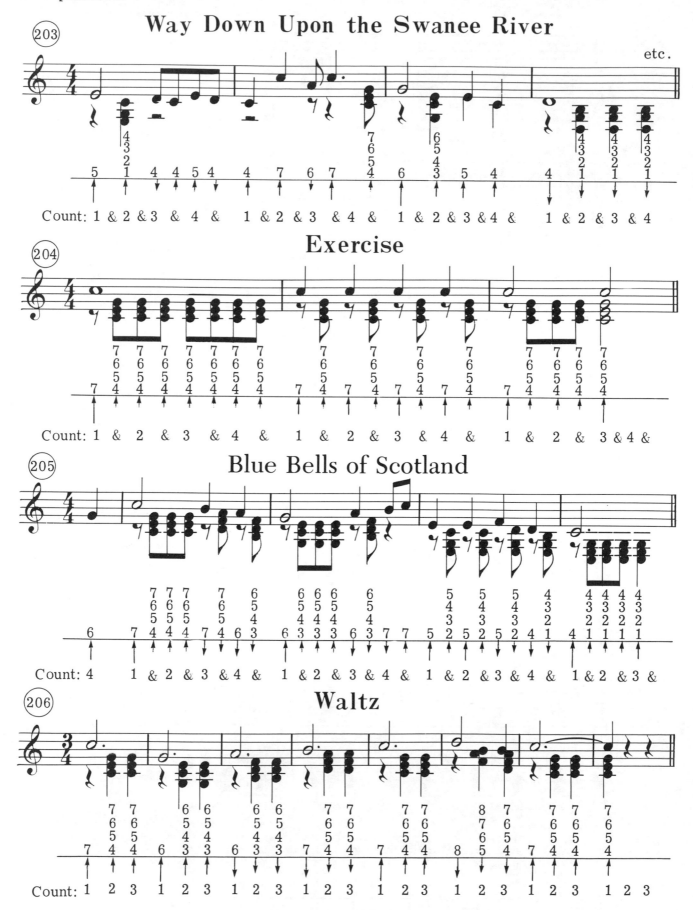

Way Down Upon the Swanee River

Exercise

Blue Bells of Scotland

Waltz

Great Music at Your Fingertips